I0670944

PASSAGES

Literature of Newfoundland and Labrador

Book 3

edited by
Eric Norman
June Warr
Ray Goulding

BREAKWATER
Canada's Atlantic Publisher

The hooked mat on the cover was made by Drucilla Smith of the Northern Peninsula. It depicts an old-time schooner on a southern voyage off Cape Norman (as indicated by the lighthouse). The canvas sails of the original schooner were brown and they were treated with a mixture of spruce and alder bark, in order to prevent rot, and it was this process which dyed the canvas.

The red airplane depicts the Grenfell Association "Mission" plane. To the people of Labrador and the Northern Peninsula this bright red "object in the sky" meant the long-awaited arrival of the doctor and nurse.

BREAKWATER wishes to acknowledge the following photographers:

Peter Ball
Ben Hansen
Justin Hall
David Wegenast/DECK'S AWASH
Jim Winter

Canadian Cataloguing in Publication Data

Main entry under title:

Passages

(Literature of Newfoundland and Labrador ; book 3)

For use in Grade 9.

ISBN: 978-0-919948-93-8

1. Canadian literature (English) — Newfoundland.*
2. Canadian literature (English) — Labrador.*
I. Norman, Eric. II. Warr, June. III. Goulding, Ray. IV. Series.

PS8255.N4S83   C810'.8'09718   C80-094851-3
PR9198.2.N42S83

© **BREAKWATER BOOKS LTD.** 1983

Reprinted 1992, 1994, 1996, 2000, 2002
Printed in Canada

TO THE TEACHER

This book is one in a series of Newfoundland literature anthologies designed for junior high school use. The need for such a series has long been felt by teachers of English in the province, and has been recognized by the Department of Education in its objectives for the English program.

Each book is arranged thematically, with some attempt to arrange works chronologically within each theme. Four major themes appear in each text. These deal with the way of life of our forebears in this country; the physical surroundings and environment in which we live; the values, attitudes and discriminations which we might see around us or experience; and the sense of community, of caring for our province, which is so much a part of our people. Minor themes appear at intervals in the three books, to bring to the attention of students our writers' treatment of other aspects of our country and people, such as our sense of humour; the place held by our province's original inhabitants; the tremendously varied and rich flora and fauna of our land; and the heroes and heroines of our people.

Our authors are drawn from the whole spectrum of Newfoundland writing, spanning geography and time. Many writers appearing in these texts have not previously been published other than in magazines or periodicals. Others are well-known and prolific. Some are polished professionals, some are talented amateurs, while others write directly and simply from the heart of experience. They all have something of value for our young people.

The format of the work is straightforward, and should help teachers present the material positively to the students. Each theme unit has a brief introduction which illuminates the aspects of the theme to be treated. Each selection within the theme has a background introduction which usually highlights as well some literary concept to be noticed in the piece. At the end of each piece is a brief biography of the author (unless the biography had appeared in an earlier selection), questions and activities which will develop further understanding of the selection, and suggestions which will help relate the literature class to other activities within the school.

Throughout the books words which may cause trouble are marked * and appear in a simple glossary at the back.

The editors suggest that classes engaged in enjoying this series should have access to at least a good wall map of the province, a library selection which includes at least the titles referred to in the series, and suitable audio-visual material available from the Department of Education, especially the series entitled "Communication Newfoundland Style." Subscriptions to Newfoundland magazines and periodicals, use of television and radio programmes with Newfoundland content, involvement in local productions by drama groups, and arranged visits to the school by local authors are all avenues which should be explored as the opportunities arise.

Each text may be treated as a unit within the regular English program, or its content may be used selectively by the teacher in an integrated approach. It is suggested, though, that material not cross over grade lines as this may lead to boredom or frustration for the student.

In choosing the selections for these texts the editors were very much aware of the reading levels and interests of the audience for which they were intended. This automatically eliminated a large part of our literature, especially that written more than fifty years ago, and practically all scholarly works. Unfortunately these factors and the restricted size of the texts also eliminated most of our drama and one or two of our major writers.

Considerable difficulty and frustration was experienced in locating literature to adequately represent Labrador. The trouble lay not so much in locating literature of Labrador as in locating writings that would be meaningful and of interest to junior high school students, and which also were written at a comprehension and vocabulary level suitable for junior high students. This proved to be a very difficult problem considering that one of our intentions in developing the series at the junior high level was to expose students in a positive way to their own literature so that enjoyment is enhanced and liking for the literature established. It is intended that more scholarly and literary approaches should be left to the high school grades. This meant that although a search was conscientiously made, Labrador literature is still not as well represented in the series as we would have liked. The same problem was encountered in this junior high series in finding suitable literature representing native peoples, ethnic groups and early chronological periods. It is our hope that these shortcomings will be corrected in material for the senior high school grades where the maturity of the student will give greater range to selection criteria.

Throughout the compilation of the series the editors were guided generally by Department guidelines and the desired outcomes which were established initially by the editorial group. It was felt that students who work positively through the series will have a good knowledge of, and pride in, their heritage, and will be readily able to see why a person with a background in this province will often have a unique point of view when dealing with issues and concerns which may be universal. They will realize that Newfoundland literature is real and legitimate literature, thinking of it in the context of literature in the English-speaking world, and they will have a good knowledge of the works and background biographies of major writers in this province, and will know something of their styles. Our students will be more alert to and appreciative of the various possibilities for take-off points for writing and acting, or for expressing themselves through the other art forms, such as painting, sketching, song or music. They will also be aware that Newfoundland literature exists in a multitude of forms, from the oral literature of folksongs to the polished work of modern writers. They will also begin to understand that dialects and patterns of speech coming to us from the past, far from being inferior things of shame, are unique and valuable in their own right, and are legitimate subjects for further study.

The series was prepared by teachers, aware that an essential ingredient for its success is the teaching which will be applied to it. We have been accustomed to thinking of the books as ours; but they are now yours as well, and we wish you much joy as you engage your students in their use.

E.N.

J.W.

R.G.

Contents

PEOPLE TOWARDS PEOPLE

PART I

No Comfort To Any Of Us

PEOPLE TOWARDS PEOPLE

PART II

Look After Number One

NATIVE PEOPLES

MARK-MAKERS

Jim Winter

A LAND OF SOME VALUE

In this unit we celebrate the love of country, the sense that we belong here, the conviction that there is no other place quite like our province. Harold Horwood pokes strong fun at those who would like to change some of our place names so that they are more like place names in other parts of Canada. Otto Kelland lets us listen to an old fisherman's love song sung to the sea and the land. Ray Guy tells us how strong were the feelings stirred in him at first sight of some of the more beautiful parts of his country. And Tom Cahill concludes the unit by showing us something of the fierce feelings aroused in Newfoundlanders who thought that something valuable was being lost by their country at the time of Confederation.

Getting Ready To Read

Although the author in this essay uses a light tone, before we read very far we realize that he does have a note of caution for us. He uses humour to get across his point-of-view, which is an important aspect of this essay. As you read the essay ask yourself what we might be losing when we modernize the names of some of our picturesque communities.

Fumigating the Map

The island of Newfoundland is justly famous for place names with a punch. Famished Gut is an example. And Rogue's Harbour. There are also Horse Chops and Hole-In-The-Wall, not to mention Sally's Leg and Virgin's Arm, all named in the distant past by sailors and fishermen with a sense of humour.

But the Post Office Department is doing its best to abolish these salty place names and to substitute such masterpieces as Port Elizabeth and Fairhaven. The improvement will be obvious, I am sure, to any fair-minded reader. We Newfoundlanders are all in favour of these improvements. We do not want to live in Hole-in-the-Wall. We want to live in Parkdale. It sounds so nice and sanitary.

We feel that if the Canada Post Office succeeds in getting rid of all the old place names we will be much the better for it. We are even prepared to help them out by supplying them with a list of old names that they've never heard of yet. At least, we are pretty certain that they have never heard of them, since they have never managed to deliver mail there. Devil's Thumb, for instance. I'll bet they've never delivered a letter to Devil's Thumb in all their born days.

And then there's Fom. That isn't really the way you spell it. On the map it is spelled "Femme", but everyone who lives there calls it Fom, so Fom it must be. There's a story about Fom.

An American yacht with a fishing party was plying along the northern inlets of Fortune Bay one evening, and tied up to a stage head in a small cove. The island off shore was known as

Petticoat Island, but the Americans didn't know that. The yachting skipper accosted* the first baccy-chewing character he met on the stage.

"Hello," he greeted. "Where are we? What do you call this settlement?"

"Fom," said the baccy-chewer, casting a speculative eye at the weather.

"OK," said the American. "We want to send a message home. Where's the telegraph office?"

"Fifteen miles out the bay," said the native, adding that they usually rowed there in a dory.

"Post Office?" said the American hopefully.

"One over in English Harbour East," the fisherman explained. "Ye must've passed it comin' along shore."

"No telegraph, no post office, no roads!" the American exclaimed. "Do you have radios here?"

"Well," the fisherman drawled, "they's a couple. But we don't turn 'em on much. Can't get the stations up in St. John's, and them Canadian fellers never seems to have any news worth while."

"Well!" exclaimed the American. "You people in Fom are really cut off from the world, aren't you?"

" 'Spose so," said the fisherman.

"Why," continued the yacht skipper, "if New York burned down tonight you wouldn't know anything about it!"

"That's true, I 'spose," the fisherman admitted, "but then," — and he paused to squirt a philosophic stream of baccy juice over the stage head — "if Fom burned down you fellers up in New York wouldn't know anything about it, either!"

You will agree that we can't have places like Fom in this day and age. The sooner they are changed to Fairhaven the better.

Our greatest misgivings are on the subject of the speed with which the Post Office is forging ahead. As a prominent politician once remarked, officialdom should never move faster than the public, but we are afraid the Post Office may be a step or two ahead of common usage here and there.

In fact, public confusion has reached the point described in an old folk tale from one of the recently renamed harbours of Fogo Island.

The tale concerns George Coles, one-time "king" of the little settlement of Hare Bay, just as his friend Henry Nipper was the unofficial "king" of neighbouring Shoal Bay.

One night after an evening of old-fashioned square dancing during which the moonshine can went round many times and everybody got very jolly, George fell asleep in his boat, tied to his own stage, in his own harbour. Some of the younger element, with a taste for practical jokes, towed the boat, George and all, to Shoal Bay, and tied it up to the stage owned by Henry Nipper.

Imagine George Cole's consternation* when he awoke in the cold and chilly light of dawn, a little shaky perhaps, in the wrong harbour, tied to the wrong stage! His reported remarks have become a classic of Newfoundland folklore:

> Who be I and where be I?
> Be I Jarge Coles or bain't I?
> Or be I Henry Nipper?
> Be I in Hare Bay or be I in Shoal Bay?
> Or have the devil got I?

The Canada Post Office will see my point, I'm sure. If things continue at their present pace we shall all, before long, be as badly off as George Coles. We won't know whether we are in Hare Bay, Shoal Bay, Ice Tickle or Happydale Acres.

I have sometimes regretted the fact that the men who originally named the Newfoundland coves cannot be present today to see how we are improving on their work. The men who built the villages of Heart's Content and Seldom-Come-By, the sailors who named Pushthrough and Run-By-Guess, the old castaway who, with a grim laugh in the teeth of fate, named Black Joke Cove — I regret that they cannot come back to see the job which the Canada Post Office is doing on those places now. They would if they could, I'm sure.

We have one little word of censure:

Among the host of lovely names with which the Post Office is redecorating the map there are a few — just a few — which strike some of us as being a doubtful improvement. We do not refer to such names as Sunnydale and Pleasantview (nobody with a pint of good red Canadian blood in his veins could object to such strikingly original names as those). No, rather we refer to such names as Pickersgillville, a settlement in Bonavista Bay named after that eminent Canadian statesman John Whitney Pickersgill.

Usually we allow statesmen to pass on to their just reward before enshrining* them on the map, and since Mr. Pickersgill is still in robust middle life I feel that this haste to embalm* him is rather indecent — like giving a man a coffin for Christmas.

Besides, I don't think Pickersgillville will last. It is too long and hard to say. People are bound to start calling it Pickersville instead. Once this process of corruption begins there is no telling where it will end. But in this case we can guess. It will be elided* to Piggersville, which is still easier to say, and from that it is but a step to Pigsville or even Pigville. It is bound to happen, and what will the Post Office do then, poor thing? It will be faced with just another ugly name, fully as bad as Famished Gut, and it will have to go through the painful process of changing it to Silverdale or something of the kind.

Harold Horwood

Harold Horwood is one of Newfoundland's most prolific and widely read writers. A partial list of his impressive literary output includes **Only the Gods Speak, White Eskimo,** *and* **Tomorrow Will Be Sunday** *— fiction;* **The Foxes of Beachy Cove** *— non-fiction;* **Beyond The Road** *— travel; and* **Bartlett, the Great Canadian Explorer** *— biography. Mr. Horwood was born in 1923 in St. John's, where he received his early education. In 1948 he joined with Joseph R. Smallwood in the campaign for Confederation with Canada. In 1951 he became the editor of the* **Evening Telegram.** *He is presently a full-time writer, being published in national and international magazines and journals. He lives in Nova Scotia with his wife and children.*

Understanding What You Have Read

1. What point does the fisherman from "Fom" make when the American yacht skipper criticizes the lack of modern communications in that community?

2. This author presents a case for *not* changing the traditional place names of Newfoundland. You present *either* an argument *for* the changes *or* some additional reasons giving more support to Horwood's argument. Make clear *your* point-of-view.

Things To Do

1. Try to find out if any of the communities near you have had name changes. In the light of what you have just read, compare the previous name with the present one.

2. You might like to read "Death of an Outport" by Al Pittman in *Baffles of Wind and Tide*.

* * *

Getting Ready To Enjoy A Song

Cape St. Mary's, located on the extreme south-western tip of the Avalon Peninsula, is today best known for its sea-bird sanctuary. But Otto Kelland's song directs our attention to the ever-shifting and changing sea environment off the cape, and the feelings it creates in the men who fish there. Notice the strong desire of the fisherman singer to be there again, his attention to detail, and his use of the senses in helping us share his feelings. Stanzas two, three and four show us the sea in different moods, each treasured and cherished by the singer. Stanza five goes beyond description and becomes a metaphor for death, while the last stanza indicates the fisherman's desire to spend eternity near the place he loves so well.

Let Me Fish Off Cape St. Mary's

Take me back — to my west-tern boat, let me fish off Cape St. Ma-ry's Where the hag — downs sail and the fog — horns wail with my friends the Browns and the Cleary's. Let me fish off Cape St. Ma—ry's

Let me feel my dory lift
To the broad Atlantic combers*
Where the tide rips swirl and the wild ducks whirl
Where Old Neptune calls the numbers
'Neath the broad Atlantic combers. . .

Let me sail up Golden Bay
With my oilskins all a'streamin'. . .
From the thunder squall — when I hauled me
trawl
And my old Cape Ann* a'gleamin'
With my oil skins all a'streamin'. . .

Let me view that rugged shore,
Where the beach is all a'glisten
With the caplin spawn where from dusk to dawn
You bait your trawl and listen
To the undertow* a'hissin'.

When I reach that last big shoal
Where the ground swells* break asunder,
Where the wild sands roll to the surges toll.
Let me be a man and take it
When my dory fails to make it.

Take me back to that snug green cove
Where the seas roll up their thunder.
There let me rest in the earth's cool breast
Where the stars shine out their wonder —
And the seas roll up their thunder.

Otto P. Kelland

Otto Kelland worked as a steward and seaman on Newfoundland ships for four years before joining the Newfoundland Police Force and serving in St. John's, Corner Brook and Bay Roberts. In 1939 he became superintendent of the St. John's prison. His best known poem is the beautiful song which you are now familiar with, but he has written numerous stories and other poems, and has published **Anchor Watch: Newfoundland Stories in Verse.**

Understanding What You Have Read

1. Explain in some detail why the singer wants to go back to the place where he fished.

2. Who is Neptune? "Old Neptune calls the numbers" suggests fatalism. What is that? Why has fatalism been a common attitude among Newfoundland fishermen?

3. The composer uses many words having "l" sounds and "s" sounds. What effect does this have on the song?

Things To Do

1. Listen to someone sing this song, or sing it yourself.

2. Find Golden Bay and Cape St. Mary's on the map. Find pictures of the area, or visit it when you have the opportunity.

3. Get a book of Newfoundland folk songs and read or sing some of the other songs which have been so popular in our province for so long.

* * *

Much of Ray Guy's work was motivated by a strong feeling for Newfoundland, his "Country." Here he highlights two parts of the province for description, telling us at the same time of his own experiences when he first visited them. As you read this short selection try to feel what the sight of Bonne Bay must have done to this "East Coaster." At Cape St. Mary's Mr. Guy was more impressed by the birds than by the sea and coastline. Try to imagine the sounds as well as the sights of that scene. You should visit both these areas when you get the opportunity. Find them on a map and determine how to get there from where you live.

A Turn In My Road

I'm not a certified nature lover. I don't get misty-eyed over trees and rivers and mountains. . .or. . . .Yes, sometimes I do and I might as well admit it. Politicians aren't the only ones who must learn to live in glass houses.

Last fall, for the first time in my life, I saw Bonne Bay. I came around a turn in the road and looked down and commenced to blubber like a baby. Despite what I'd heard about it, and the pictures and the movies, I hadn't expected it to be like that.

Suddenly I was richer than I had thought and I was living in a greater Country than I had thought. It meant a good deal more to be a Newfoundlander.

Pride is said to be a sin. But the second thing I thought about was how good it would be to show someone from "upalong" — whether an exiled relative or mainland visitor — around Bonne Bay.

"This is part of the land your parents were born in, Cousin. Nothing to be ashamed of, what?" Or "Take a look, dear fellow Canadian, and see if you can think of any Newfie jokes."

I have travelled a little in eastern North America and there are two things I have seen in Newfoundland that impress me more than palm trees, the Empire State Building, the CN Tower, or the Pentagon parking lot . . . even after I made generous allowance for natural bias.

One is the astounding spectacle of the bird rocks at Cape St. Mary's. I was down for part of a day last summer and it is ahead of most things I've seen. Birds by the thousands and thousands. Gannets, gulls, puffins, turrs. Squawking and screeching and wheeling and diving to make you giddy.

The other is the country in the Bonne Bay area.

Bonne Bay and environs is the last little corner of the island that hasn't been skinned out and despoiled. It is hard for anyone who has not seen it to imagine it.

Most Newfoundlanders live on the eastern part of the island and have never seen the west coast. But many of them probably know Terra Nova National Park.

This park has pleasant salt water indrafts and rolling hills covered by scrubby spruce. It is relatively small in area.

Multiply the little bog-spruce patch of Terra Nova by one hundred and you have Bonne Bay.

How many thousands of tourists visit Terra Nova Park each year? How many Newfoundlanders have taken their visitors there with pride? Multiply Terra Nova by a hundred and you have Bonne Bay. Multiply it by thousands and you have Bonne Bay as it could be in the future.

I'm not a certified nature lover, but I believe I'll go back to that turn in the road again to make sure it's all still there.

Ray Guy

Ray Guy is a widely-read Newfoundland journalist. Since the early 1960s, he has written for local newspapers and magazines, and more recently has appeared regularly in mainland publications. He has won two national awards for his writing, the most recent being the Stephen Leacock Award for Humour for **That Far Greater Bay** *published in 1976.*

Mr. Guy is a native of Arnold's Cove and is presently living in St. John's with his wife and children. Aside from his writing, Mr. Guy will be known to students as Jack, a character appearing in the CBC television series "Up At Ours."

Understanding What You Have Read

1. Can you suggest why Ray Guy insists that he is not "a certified nature lover"?

2. How does the first sight of Bonne Bay affect Mr. Guy? Do you think that has anything to do with his wanting to go back?

3. Do you know if anything has happened in Bonne Bay which would support Ray Guy's predictions in his last paragraphs?

Things To Do

1. Ray Guy seems concerned that the beauty of his "Country" be recognized and shared by others. Can you support this by reference to his essay?

2. Try to get pictures of the Bird Rocks. Better still, try to get a recording of the sounds at the sanctuary.

3. If you don't live in Bonne Bay try to get some pictures or film of the area.

* * *

Getting Ready To Read

The setting for Tom Cahill's play "As Loved Our Fathers" is the kitchen of Con and Trese Hartrey. The time is 1948, when Newfoundlanders were trying to decide whether they wished to become Canadians.

In the first excerpt you witness Con's reaction after hearing that his wife and mother-in-law have voted for Confederation and his brother-in-law has supported Commission government.

The second excerpt takes place on the day of the second referendum. Mel (Imelda Roberts, Trese's cousin who is a school teacher) has been accused by Con of allowing a letter from the Orange Lodge to influence how she has voted.

As Loved Our Fathers

CON: See, you're just like your brother there. When someone finally comes up with an argument that convinces you, you justs backs away and says "Oh, it's no use arg'in'." I'm stating a case. You're giving this country away for a baby bonus, because you're too stunned, both of you, to think about what's really going to happen to you!

GORD: (Changing his pillow and legs from upstage to down)
Look out, he's getting wound up again!

CON: Sure I'm getting wound up. Somebody's got to get wound up around here. Don't you see what's happened to Newfoundland all along? We're either too soft or too stunned, it's hard to figure out which. You weren't allowed to settle here for the first hundred years because the overseas merchants wanted to keep all the goodies for themselves. They figured settlers were nothing but trouble, wanting land grants and concessions* and finally to run the show themselves. So we had to hide away in the coves, and look what that did to us. Turned us into half-starved criminals, scrabbling to make a living. Kept us from getting together and making something of the place. And when we finally did get our own government, our own crowd turned it into a circus, and they took it away from us, and turned us back into a colony again. And now we have the chance! Now we have money in the bank, educated. young people, and enough importance to go to any country in the world and say we've got something to offer. And this is the very time people like you want to make us a colony again. Because, it was bad enough being a colony of England, but if we joins Canada tonight, in twenty years we'll be a colony again, a colony of Ottawa and Toronto. Who wouldn't get wound up when half the people in Newfoundland is willing to sell us up the St. Lawrence river for thirty dollars a month for that old woman, and your precious baby bonus?

GORD: Ah, what's the difference who we joins, we'll all be dead soon, anyway. Come on, let's go down to Bennett's and hear some returns.

† † †

MEL: (Giving Trese a return hug as she hangs on her shoulder, then stepping past her to face Con) Don't cry, Trese. Don't let him make you cry! (She advances to face him across the table.) Now you listen to me, Con Hartrey! You've known me, grew up with me in the same harbour among the same few hundred people for forty years. And if you think I'd change my mind about something I care for as much as this island because a piece of garbage like that came in the mail, then I haven't much respect for you either! That thing is nothing but a cheap political trick, put out by people not much better than the ones who'll believe it or do what it says! And it's you and your kind are as much responsible for it as the ones who put it out! Because you made it necessary! You rooted around until you could find some people who'd get down in the gutter with you, and you found them! You live on that sickening drivel! You thrive on it like maggots on a dead fish! And it's what ruined Newfoundland before and drove her to the wall in '32. Bigotry* and selfishness! Grab what you can for yourself and your gang and forget the people who need something! There's only one thing we can be sorry for tonight. Now the people might never know what they really wanted to do. And they might never realize how they really felt when they were asked to give up everything they loved. And that's because of people like you and the crowd that sent that letter! (She walks to the door and opens it before turning back.) If only half the people who vote tonight will do it because they want someone else besides themselves to have something, then maybe we've learned a lesson. And if that means Confederation, then let's have Confederation! (She is gone with a slam of the door. Trese looks about, terrified by the long pause.)

Tom Cahill

Tom Cahill's **As Loved Our Fathers** *has received wide acclaim, but it was not his first success in drama. He wrote a stage version of Harold Horwood's* **Tomorrow Will Be Sunday** *which won many major awards in the 1967 Dominion Drama Festival. He presently works as a producer with CBC Television in St. John's. One of his most interesting productions has been the series "Where Once They Stood"* *which deals with the history and culture of various Newfoundland communities. Mr. Cahill was born in St. John's in 1929, and received his education there. In 1955 he moved to Corner Brook to work as a reporter, columnist, cartoonist and associate editor of the* **Western Star**, *before joining the CBC.*

Understanding What You Have Read

1. Empathy is the ability to share the feelings of another. Try to separate the logic from the emotion in what Con and Mel say; then put yourself in each of their places and say how you think each felt at that time. Try to have empathy with each of them.

Things To Do

1. Read the entire play "As Loved Our Fathers."

2. Ask your history teacher to discuss the alternatives given to Newfoundlanders in 1948.

* * *

Jim Winter

Justin Hall

Justin Hall

Peter Ball

OUR ENVIRONMENT

The selections in this unit give us descriptions of four different parts of our environment, a storm, a town, a seascape and a wild animal.

Tom Dawe describes a scene which we know only too well: the brooding quiet which forecasts a storm in winter. John Mitchell paints for us the numerous activities and scenes in one of our more picturesque and busy towns. The fury of wind and rain in summer, and images of sea and sun fill the poem by Michael Wade. And Donald Dodds brings us into the woods and marshlands to let us look through very observant eyes at the wildlife to be found there.

This unit presents a mosaic of our surroundings.

Getting Ready To Read

"Storm Coming, Winter Afternoon" is a lyric poem. It describes the sights seen through the window of a house. In describing the winter afternoon scene, the poet creates a sombre, dreary mood, which is the effect of the winter scene on the speaker.

One device the poet uses to aid him in describing the details of the scene is the simile. Similes are very common in everyday speech; for instance, "he's as fat as a bear" or "her eyes shone like diamonds." While these similes have been used so often they are worn out, the similes a poet uses are usually very fresh and striking. Tom Dawe in "Storm Coming, Winter Afternoon" uses "three crows drifting ... like discarded gloves" as a striking and meaningful simile. As you read the poem, appreciate the use of similes in the description the poet writes, and how they aid in the creation of the mood of the poem.

Storm Coming, Winter Afternoon

Three crows drifting on the windy sky
like discarded gloves
fall suddenly
into the hazy woods
far beyond a well-house
with a swinging door
that blinks dark openings.

Out in the frozen yard
a clothesline pole
swings back and forth
like a wild metronome.*
Only the stalks of the cut grass
seem to be still.

Across the vapor fields
that once waved with August,

the thirsty scythe-men
used to wave at me
as they came to the well-house
with cool white jugs
and noons above the clothesline pole;
one of them once stopped
and read my birthday book to me:
a fable from Aesop
about a crow, smooth pebbles,
and a water-pitcher....

Now I cannot see the woods
through the massing snowflakes
and the well-house is lost
somewhere out there.
I hear the clothesline straining
at its rusty pulleys
like something animate* and suffering.
Near my window
I watch the grass stalks
rigid in the shifting hollows.

Tom Dawe

Tom Dawe has won awards in the Newfoundland and Labrador Arts and Letters Competition for his short stories, poems, plays and sketches. This Newfoundland artist was born in 1940 at Long Pond, Manuels in Conception Bay. He has published numerous articles, poems and stories, and has written extensively for radio. Collections of his poems have been published in **Hemlock Cove and After, In A Small Cove,** *and* **Connections.** *He is presently a member of the English faculty of Memorial University in St. John's.*

Understanding What You Have Read

1. The secret of writing a good description is to include many details in the scene. What details does the poet include in his description?

2. What is the difference in time in stanza three and time in the other three stanzas?

3. Who was Aesop? What was his fable about the "crow, smooth pebbles, and a water-pitcher"?

Things To Do

1. a) Write the similes used in "Storm Coming, Winter Afternoon."
   b) Write three original similes of your own.

2. a) Explain what is meant by "swinging door that blinks".
   b) What are the "dark openings"?
   c) What effect does the picture "dark openings" have on you?

* * *

Jim Winter

Getting Ready To Read

This free verse poem uses a "stream of consciousness" technique; that is, the poet allows a number of images to flow with little connecting action. The images appeal strongly to the senses, with action suggested but not completed.

The author is not a resident of the town, but is connected to it through his ancestry.

Grand Bank, Newfoundland

tar melting day
banker's fleet gone
tibbo and son
buffett and forsey
old signs, pale

glossy draggers
scourges

ocean squeezed up
in a net

kids hooking eel
their wicked
neck and eye
poured out
a few inches
below timbers
of the kelped wh

kids
hop and skip

on the grump* head
catch the skeptic*
head
with silver jig

two death eyes
bloody a wharf

waiting gulls
shriek
their wages of wings
beat and float
hover
waiting for updrafts
to sweep skyward

I know I was sent here
to see these things
to return to my own world
for a summer
to find the interval
between the dying sea
coloured oil
and the sky full
of bright wings
pounding down
for strangled guts
biting and squawking
insanely
And I am glad

I am caught up in their wings

John Mitchell

John S. Mitchell was born in 1944 in St. John's. He is now living near Montreal and teaching at Dawson College. He has written one book of poetry, **Eyes That Shamed The Light**, *which was published in 1972.*

Understanding What You Have Read

1. The title is specific. Can you supply a more general one?

2. Why does the author say he is glad?

Things To Do

1. If you don't live in or near Grand Bank, try to get pictures of the area. Find it on the map.

2. Find out what each of the following is:

   a) banker's fleet
   b) grump head
   c) dragger

* * *

Getting Ready To Read

Authors often give inanimate objects human characteristics. This is known as personification. Watch how the author personifies nature in the following poem.

The Rain Hammers

The rain hammers at my window
    with fists abandoned by the wind
    my curtains billow with delight
    at the curious black waters bludgeoning*

inside
    a semi-precious bumblebee
    mysteriously hums above
    a plastic flower

eternity becomes
    the sound of the sea in the night
    the pound of the tide in the black
    the flood of the shore in the dark
    the cry of the gull in the dawn

the sun comes out of the sea
    covered with weed
    surrounded with sound
    cornered by clouds
    and breathes on the world.

Michael Wade

Michael Wade was born in Avondale in the early 1940s and is an English graduate of Memorial University. He published his first poem in 1972 in **Voices Underground**, *a magazine edited by Harold Horwood. Besides being a creative writer he is also an accomplished musician. Mr. Wade has moved to Nova Scotia and is presently writing a novel.*

Understanding What You Have Read

1. Quote several examples from the poem to illustrate the human personality of nature.

2. Although this poem makes no open reference to Newfoundland, we feel strongly that it refers to our environment. What other provinces might feel just as strongly that it speaks of them? Why?

Things To Do

1. Read "Newfoundland" by E.J. Pratt. You will see similar personification of nature if you read Tom Dawe's "The Madonna" in *Baffles of Wind and Tide*.

2. Write a short paragraph saying what "type of person" nature seems to be in this poem.

* * *

Getting Ready To Read

The author of this selection, a wildlife biologist, is well qualified to describe the plant and animal life of this province. But Donald Dodds has more than knowledge. Notice his skill in description, his attention to detail, and how his descriptions appeal to the senses. Notice too that his affection for the animals allows him to give individual personalities to them, and that this device grasps and holds our interest.

Vulpes, The Fox

All round the potato field above the brook the roots are piled high. Young cherry and birch grow from the topsoil in the debris and, with the roots and stumps, form a fence. Now the field is covered with hard-packed snow, granular beneath the morning crust. In the afternoon the crust melts and the prints of animals appear. Dog and cat have walked across this field. Other creatures with different prints pad the field at night on the frozen crust. Ice crystals reflect sunlight from the tracks of the nocturnal* lynx and fox.

Deletrix is on the forest side of the fence moving towards her root-den. She carries a snowshoe rabbit, warm and limp. Its rear leg muscles jerk to answer impulses not yet dead. Within the natal den five yet-blind cubs lie together, fur balls apparently without noses and without ends to their tails. At the bitch fox's entrance, the balls will uncurl and the young will nurse as the mother feeds on the rabbit.

Yesterday there were six young. One, the smallest and weakest, Deletrix carried away and covered with sticks, abandoning it to death.

Gojavick, the male fox, is hunting. He had hunted food for the female for two weeks and is not aware that his restless mate has left her cubs for a while. From now on she will hunt more.

Each day, as the snow melts, light increases within the den. When the cubs are eighteen days old, tiny slits appear across their eyes. Three days later the slits see light and play begins.

Though the parents are careful in their approach to the

birth chamber, they are seen. The farmer, who has lost a chicken, takes care to watch the back fields. With his son, he moves to dig out the young.

"You tink de bitch is in 'er?" the son asks.

"I don't know, gimme dat pick and we'll soon find out if she's 'ere."

The two men shovel and pick. The boy returns to the farm for a bar to pry rocks and an axe to chop roots.

"Wished we 'ad dynamite, skipper. A stick of dynamite 'ud do 'er."

The older man nodded. "We'll get 'em!" he said.

Deletrix watched from a distance of only a few yards. Gojavick was away hunting. He had returned to a small grass marsh for more meadow mice for the young. Yesterday he found several remaining from the winter's hardships and had brought three into the chamber.

Inside the den, the little foxes move towards the opening and the noise, hesitantly, then back away trembling. Their eyes and ears are alert. The smell is strange. But there is no one to guide them and they do not know what to do.

"What we gonna do wid 'em, skipper?"

"We'll club 'em and leave 'em and den watch an' de old lady'll be back sure and we'll shoot 'er."

And they dig until the nest is bared and swing with shovel and pick at the kits and Deletrix moves. Like a flash she speeds between the killers, only a foot away from either. Her piercing shriek frightens the men who hesitate too long, and one kit, Vulpes, escapes. The men move for their gun, but the bitch and her pup are away.

Vulpes travels with his mother all summer. He learns to hunt and meets often with Gojavick who carries food for him. It is a playful life for Vulpes, even without his brothers and sisters, for he plays with Deletrix the mother, with leaves and sticks, and most often with his own tail.

He likes to dig and push his nose into the soft earth as far as it will go, and he uses it to cover bones and debris. This is how Deletrix stores food, and Vulpes copies her.

Vulpes moves away from his mother and travels short distances by himself as the summer wanes. He spends many hours lying lazily in the sun, catching grasshoppers and young birds learning to fly. Late summer is a time of gradual parting for the bitch and her cub. November finds Deletrix far away from the farm area. Vulpes seldom sees her.

Winter brings hardship for all animals. Many will lose weight as the weather becomes cold. Vulpes has grown a heavy red coat to protect himself from the frost and when he wakens from his snow-bed the moisture clings, frozen to the tips of his guard-hair. The woolly under-fur of grey insulates his body and there is little loss of heat.

Foxes kill and steal to live, though most would rather steal. Vulpes hunts mice and plays with them after they are caught. When little birds come close the fox fools them by pretending he does not see them. Early in the winter Vulpes visits the farms and searches out the buildings carefully, but each visit makes him wilder and less bold.

His greatest thrill is chasing Lepus the hare. Lepus runs in great leaps and turns sharply to avoid being caught. To Lepus the chase means escape and life and he soars as if on wings above the branches normally passed under. Into the dense second-growth fir the hare glides, but he knows cover alone will not protect him from Vulpes the fox. One moment Vulpes is a calculating missile of the wilderness waiting to fire at a point he expects Lepus to pass. The next moment Vulpes is the orange flame streaking across the alder-bed and into the firs. Vulpes does not always catch the hare but this time he is successful, for the fir is not dense enough to prevent Vulpes' lightning-like movements close to the ground. If there were a few more inches of snow, the maze of lower branches would slow the fox's movements, or, if the fir growth were younger and bushier close to the snow line, perhaps the hare would live. Lepus screams as the fox grabs his back and holds for seconds before dropping him for a better grip at the base of the neck. Vulpes clamps the hare's neck strongly and throws the animal, with a snap of his head. Into the snow fluff the hare falls on its side. Lepus's hind legs move, but he has a broken neck and his final escape is death itself.

In February Vulpes sits one night in the light new snowfall. For many days he has felt restless, less inclined to hunt but more inclined to move. It is nearing mid-month. Vulpes cries out. He barks several times and then lies down, whimpers, and 'winds' the winter air with keen sense of smell. Far away on a distant knoll a second fox cries as if in answer. Mating time has arrived.

The nocturnal barking continues for several nights. Vulpes travels far during the dark hours and barks from several hills each night. During the day he sleeps.

It is mid-February when Vulpes finds his mate. She is a young animal, like Vulpes, and approaches her first breeding time. Together they travel across the frozen, moonlit crust, leaving prints side by side and overlapping in the hoarfrost — tracks that will be gone with the first tongues of sun.

The foxes mate five days after their meeting. They travel and hunt together and then go two miles away from their hunting-grounds to the great burned-over area blessed with hollow logs for foxes. They examine several den-sites before choosing a fallen forest monarch, hollow to the tip.

Vulpes is carrying sticks about in his mouth now and litters the log floor with his burdens. His mate moves less, mainly depending on the male to bring her food.

Fifty-one days from their time of mating, the bitch gives birth to six cubs. Two are grey-black and four are grey-yellow. As they grow, the two dark ones will become silver foxes. The yellowish ones will cover their wool with red-orange guard-hair. Vulpes hunts very hard for the bitch and the cubs. Rabbits have suddenly become scarce and he must take many small birds to augment* the rabbit diet. There is much carrion* in this country from the fall hunting season and the parts of carcasses left by poachers, but foxes are cautious of the dead.

Vulpes' nose, keen enough to discern bits of flesh beneath several feet of frozen snow, tells him of a dead animal not far from the den. Sitting on a stump a few feet from the den-entrance, he watches in the early morning. Ravens pick at a moose carcass recently bared as the snow melted. The object was seen by the carrion-feeders from the great dead trees, spires of the clearing, and now they feed. The birds stay with the carcass for two or three days and then Vulpes investigates, only to find the rib-cage on the top picked white and clean.

Beneath, the ribs still lie partly frozen and the ravens and crows have worked with less success. It is midnight and the moon outlines the little dog, tail humped, scratching, biting, and tearing to loosen the meat bones from the partly frozen earth. He is successful and the cubs will eat.

In May the bitch moves her cubs to another den-site. Now the young play about the entrance and sometimes move away. Each strange object is a lesson in caution and the cubs learn quickly.

Vulpes pays less attention to his family as they grow older, though he constantly returns to visit or bring some new-found carrion, or a rabbit. He hunts alone at night, returning to his former haunts, shying away from man or his tracks, jumping high over trails where man has passed.

At night he sits on the edge of a log watching the shadowy moose walk across the open. A faint, low howl begins, repeating itself, higher and louder, and suddenly ends. It is the lynx, Cervier, calling from the forest on the other side of the bog marsh. Vulpes does not move. Though lynx and fox compete for the same foods, they are not enemies. Many times Vulpes has been close to the lynx, though the cat has not been aware of the dog's presence. Vulpes' nose is sharp. Cervier's sight is keen but his nose is dull. The lynx cry does not arouse Vulpes' curiosity. He is indifferent. Yet at the second cry he stands, slowly turns, and trots away, then stops and barks a shivering cry as if to answer Cervier before he sinks into the forest.

September is a wonderful time of the year to Vulpes. Nights are cool and his new growing coat protects him during the chilly hours. A month ago he was a woolly, ragged creature looking gaunt and thin. Now he is a new fox. This is the time of year for berries. Since August he has fed on raspberries and partridge berries as well. Marsh cranberries hold on even until spring and now sprinkle the bogs with tiny red-pepper dots. Vulpes feeds and fattens. A fox adds to his meat diet anything that he can find. In the spring, grasses are good. In the summer, insects; and in the fall, berries. So now he travels to the barrens above the timber slopes.

Vulpes sits on a brown rock in the middle of the clearing. It is early morning and blueberries that grow in abundance in the acid sub-soil fill the fox's belly to roundness. A moose appears and Vulpes crouches low. He does not fear the moose and when his nose has determined there is no alien smell he will sit up again. Soon a second moose, a third, and a fourth appear. They are bulls and they gather for a purpose. A great male with giant antlers approaches. This is Alces. Each animal challenges the huge bull. Antlers are placed together and each strives to shove the other backwards. The half-ton creatures snort heavily and cough as they strain to force Alces back. Four try and fail. As each animal tries, the others watch. At first curious, then eager to join the fight, Vulpes jumps to the ground and prances toward Alces. The giant moose eyes the dog fox and waves his mighty antlers at the dodging fur menace. Vulpes squeals with pleasure and challenges again. He dodges gracefully away at each swerve of Alces' antlers. Suddenly he is attacked from behind as a shadow closes over him. A second bull wishes to strike at the little dancing dog. Vulpes dashes quickly out of the great deer circle and cautiously creeps around them, eyeing the group with short, sweeping glances, yet unconcernedly. The bulls watch the fox until their dim eyesight can no longer discern movement.

Man is everywhere in the wind some days. Vulpes travels farther into the forests to avoid him. Deletrix has returned to man to steal. This has been her life and becomes the cause of her death.

In the next green spring the great log contains six kits. Two are dark. Four are light. The bitch nurses the young. Vulpes hunts again for his mate.

Donald G. Dodds

Donald G. Dodds was born in the United States but has spent most of his adult life in Canada. He worked for a time as wildlife biologist and consultant for the Newoundland Government. His observations and experiences in the field provided the material for **Wild Captives** *which was published in 1965. Since then his expertise has been employed by the United Nations, the Canadian Government, and agencies in Rome, Kenya and Zambia. Dr. Dodds has published numerous papers, short stories and scripts.*

Understanding What You Have Read

1. What do you think of Dodd's treatment of human characters as compared to animal characters?

2. This selection is from *Wild Captives,* a book dealing with animals and men in Newfoundland. Think about that title, and try to explain why the naturalist selected it for his book.

Something To Do

1. Read *The Biography of a Silver Fox* by Ernest T. Seton.

* * *

David Wegenast / *DECK'S AWASH*

FOREBEARS

PART I

All Without Television

These selections illustrate for us how people managed before the days of the mass media. The place of games, songs and stories in the lives of our forebears cannot be overestimated. They not only entertained, but were also educational. In some cases they allowed for the sharing of feelings too deep to be borne alone.

Art Scammell tells us how men created a game and learned something about their country and themselves in the process. Daniel Endicott sings a ghost song, just as hundreds of other songs like it were sung for entertainment in days gone by. Len Margaret tells a ghost story which shares elements of Mr. Endicott's song. And then a man brags about his dog before telling us a true hunting story. But his hunting story has echoes in hundreds of other hunting and fishing adventures related over the years in countless stages, camps and kitchens. Victor Butler's tragic story has the personal touch of the oral tradition of story telling, involving the listener in gripping feeling for him.

Getting Ready To Read

In reading about Mr. Scammell's Mock Parliament (formed from his fellow Orange Lodge members) try to visualize the dramatic situation which he describes. His descriptions of the local men in their everday attire taking over such important positions as Minister of Justice and Minister of Finance provide a sharp contrast which has its own built-in humour. With no television and very little in the way to entertain them, these folk improvised and provided their own entertainment. At the same time that we see the fun in this essay, we are also keenly aware of the fact that these men (untrained in politics) could, no doubt, do the job as well as, if not better than, the men already holding the actual portfolios in government.

My Political Career

About 35 years ago I was teaching in a small outport in Newfoundland when I was suddenly catapulted* into politics. There was an Orange Lodge in the place and thinking that by joining I could enter more fully into the social life of the community I sent in my name to become a member. I joined.

One winter night after we had finished our business we were all racking our brains for something to enliven the proceedings. In an unguarded moment I suggested that we hold a mock parliament. At that time political interest was very keen and everybody from the Master of the Lodge to the Tyler instantly showed great enthusiasm for the idea. We had a good crowd there that night and prospects of a ready-made political career without the bug-bear of elections seized us. None of us knew the first thing about it, but being Newfoundlanders we were used to improvising. Never in the political annals of our country, or of any other country, was there a government formed in such a hurry, or with more disregard for parliamentary protocol.*

The Tories were in power at that time so I was elected Tory Prime Minister by everybody, including the potential opposition, and given ten minutes to form a Cabinet. The

Customs Officer, a man of lion courage, boldly risked his job by agreeing to be Leader of the Opposition. In the fever of the moment we even forgot to enquire if he had been successful in the last elections. For all we knew or cared he might not have saved his nomination fee.

On my mettle,* with the fate of the country trembling in my inexperienced hands, I hurriedly looked over my political material and made some split-second decisions.

"Uncle Bill Glover," I yelled, singling out the only man in the harbour who owned a codtrap, "you take Marine and Fisheries."

"Right you are, your honour," growled Uncle Bill, loosening his muffler and hooking a small squid-jigger bottom up in his turtle-neck sweater as a badge of office.

Henry Knight, the mailman, was a natural for Minister of Posts and Telegraphs.

Bill Searle was on the local school board so I made sure of our school grant by giving him the Education portfolio. For an amateur I was learning fast. I might want the school again the following year. After all, this political job mightn't last out the night. I noticed Bill combing his hair on the sly and putting up a hand to straighten a tie that he'd left home.

I asked the local merchant, Jim Squires, to be my Minister of Finance. Jim was pretty hard-headed about handing out favours, as he had to be to keep his business afloat in those days. At first I had been seriously considering Skipper John Parsons for the job. John was a Justice of the Peace and had some little means. But he was a bit too free for watch dog of the Treasury, I figured. He had a delightful habit of turning up at the annual Sunday School picnic with a huge bag of peppermint knobs and scattering them with lavish hand all over the "green" to be pounced on by cheering youngsters. I saw in my mind's eye John's big, generous hand dipping, not into a bag of candy but into the government chest. I shuddered and Skipper John, J.P., became my new Minister of Justice. He would, I knew, temper* it with mercy.

By this time my ten minutes were just about up according to the dollar watch given me by the school-youngsters at Christmas. I quickly completed my Cabinet and we lined up the chairs on opposite sides of the House. We had some difficulty in getting the members seated. Two members of the Opposition had already bummed a pipeful of Edgeworth tobacco each from my Minister of Finance, and my own Posts and Telegraphs was badgering him for money to buy a new leader for his dog team. Trying to live up to his new important role in the national economy, Jim had temporarily thrown off his strict business habits. He was promising loans, squaring accounts and generally heading straight for bankruptcy when the Speaker of the House, tall, slim Peter Courtney, the tidewaiter,* called the House to order. And high time too. He just saved Posts and Telegraphs from giving away his job as mailman to Opposition member Joe Bursey who had been doggedly, but unsuccessfully sending in tenders for it to the government for the past ten years.

I rescued my Cabinet and we squared away for debate. The Leader of the Opposition started off with a blistering attack on my government's agricultural policy, especially taking us to task for the bad seed potatoes we had distributed the previous spring. The pent-up resentment of months was in his speech and we had to sit and take it. Imagine my horror and consternation when I heard my Minister of Agriculture and Mines joining loudly in the hear, hears of approval. Big Jake Carroll had forgotten that that was his responsibility. He was remembering only the poor potato crop and the canker in the government imported spuds that had caused it. I hurriedly scribbled a note and passed it along the line to him. He opened it and read, "Jim, shut your big mouth. In a few minutes you have to get up and answer that rat satisfactorily or your job is gone and you'll be back with an old black punt and a killick,* trawling tomcods." That fixed the hear, hears from him. He got up in his turn and did a masterly job of justification for himself and us in his maiden speech, making up in vehemence what he lacked in logic. The Speaker had quite a job getting him to speak of his attacker as "my honourable opponent." Jim had some more colorful adjectives thought up and his Cabinet colleagues were contributing others to him freely in loud whispers. But I was agreeably surprised by his political astuteness.* He succeeded in shifting all the blame for the poor seed across the Gulf onto the Prince Edward Islanders.

"How was I to know," thundered Agriculture and Mines, "that our order for seed potatoes was going to turn out like that? I put in four barrels myself and you all know what I got out in the fall. Just enough to feed one small pig till Old Christmas Day. When I killed 'un he was so lean I had to go to the Minister of Finance there and buy good salt pork to fry 'un in. Didn't I Jim?" This dire reversal of fortune enlisted the heart-felt sympathy of both sides of the House and Jake sat down, a martyr to Newfoundland agriculture, with his skin-booted feet fixed firmly on the first rung of the political ladder.

Foiled in their first dastardly attempt on us, the Opposition rallied their forces and attacked next our most vulnerable ministry, Fisheries. Uncle Bill Glover's face was getting redder and redder, I noticed, as he winced under the barrage of sarcasm and invective hurled against his department. His bonus scheme on vessel-building, the cull* on fish, the bad drying weather — it was all blamed on poor old Uncle Bill, and my heart bled for the honest old sea-dog who was getting hotter under the collar all the time. Two of my non-Cabinet men were so overcome by the eloquence of the Opposition that they tried to cross the House. We yanked them back to the Tory bench after a miniature tug-of-war with our gleeful opponents and the debate went on. I tried to catch Uncle Bill's eye to give him a heartening wink but couldn't, as he was trying to shed his big home-knit turtle-neck sweater with his pipe still in his mouth. Justice was helping him, but some hot ashes had fallen into the sweater and it was beginning to smoulder. All political differences were forgotten and the Speaker hurriedly called a recess until we could put out the fire in our Fisheries Department.

My Finance Minister took advantage of the diversion to confer with his Prime Minister, meaning me.

"Suppose they ask me to bring down the budget?" he queried nervously.

"Bring it down," I said. "It has to come down sometime. Might as well be tonight. Here, wait a minute. I'll scratch down a few figures on the back of this old school bill."

I hurriedly concocted some figures, giving Education a

princely sum and earmarking* it plainly for teachers' salaries.

"Better let the other ministers see this before the House resumes sittings," I continued. After all it would never do to have my own Ministers arguing about the budget after it was read and saying they'd never seen it before. I wanted to limit the argument if possible to what would come from the other side. Next I had a few words with Uncle Bill Glover and gave him a few points on answering the attack on Fisheries. Uncle Bill's sterling qualities were not what was needed in this game of mental gymnastics, and I knew his defence would not be a strong one. Suddenly, I heard my Agriculture Minister arguing hotly with Jim Squires, the merchant.

"Look here, Mr. Squires, 1 want another $100,000.00 to try out better breeds in sheep and cows. It's nothing out of your pocket."

Jim grinned. He was beginning to enjoy this. He had had to turn down Jake's request for $25.00 credit in his store the day before and it tickled him to hear Jake talking in the hundred thousands. He rubbed his chin reflectively.

"Well, Jake, I don't know. I might let you have $50,000.00 or so but I'll have to take it off somewhere else. Guess it'll have to come off Education. You know you didn't have that much to spend last year."

It was Jake's turn to laugh. "You should know. When I squared my account you didn't leave me much to spend."

After the House reopened, Uncle Bill handled the debate on Fisheries rather lamely and then we brought down the budget. Sniping from the Opposition couldn't have been more intense if the figures had been real.

Criticizing the Fishery estimates, one of our opponents wanted to know if there was anything in them providing for a "groaner" (bell-buoy) on Jerry's Rock just around the point of the harbour.

"That sunker is dangerous," he emphasized, "I've struck my boat's skig* there more than once."

Public Works came in for a flood of requests and Jim Squires had to keep revising his figures for that department to take care of wells, bridges and wharves. He had to get the loan of another stub of pencil from Posts and Telegraphs, and the original budget made out on my used school bill had spread to cover a page torn from the Lodge minute book (the last one), the backs of four fish receipts (contributed by Finance) and an old Custom entry form (donated by the Opposition Leader).

It was 12 o'clock by the time we had all our paper used up and that was too late to start on the Dog Act, although the Minister of Agriculture who had three sheep killed by Posts and Telegraph's mail-dogs, threatened to resign unless something was done. He was mollified* by the promise of a job as messenger boy for his son as soon as the post became vacant and everybody heaved a sigh of relief. We were all exhausted physically and mentally. In my closing speech I struck a serious note for education, pointing out that every Newfoundland child should have the chance to be thoroughly equipped to discuss public matters intelligently and that I was sure the night's experience had proven this to be no easy accomplishment. (Hear, hears from exhausted statesmen on all sides of the House.) We closed by singing "God Save the King" and I crossed the House to shake hands with the Leader of the Opposition.

Art Scammell

Mr. Arthur Scammell was born on Change Islands and spent his early years there, near the squid jigging ground about which he wrote his famous song. He was educated at Change Islands and St. John's before moving to Montreal where he taught school for over twenty years. He finished his teaching career on the faculty of Memorial University's English Department.

Mr. Scammell has written for various publications, and co-founded the regional periodical **The Atlantic Guardian.** *His writing includes songs, ballads, poems, essays and short stories.*

He is a frequent guest speaker around the province, and a welcome guest in many high school English classes. Mr. Scammell and his wife now reside in St. John's.

Understanding What You Have Read

1. The men became more serious in the mock parliament than Mr. Scammell expected them to be. Support this by reference to the story. Why did that happen?

2. What were some of the obvious problems with Mr. Scammell's government? How did his ministers contend with the problems?

Things To Do

1. Note the difficult vocabulary in places and be sure to look up the meaning of any word with which you have trouble.

2. Enlist your teacher's help to set up a Mock Parliament in your own class. Debate some present-day issues.

* * *

Getting Ready to Enjoy a Song

Everyone enjoys a ghost story, especially if it seems to have an element of truth in it. Here's one about ghosts on George's Bank, a fishing ground south of Newfoundland much frequented by our fishermen. It seems rather strange that most of the songs about that area are ghost songs, or songs about tragedies. Mr. James Gillespie, from whose singing the tune was recorded, claimed in 1929 that he had seen the ghostly seamen, and that the ship which they had boarded never sailed again because no crew would man her, and she rotted at her berth in St. John's harbour. The song describes the boarding, and we get the feeling that the composer is quite serious in his tale.

Notice that the song is in ballad form, and is addressed directly to the listeners. The storyteller actually interrupts himself at one point to ask us to be patient and let him continue.

This song is taken from a collection by Elisabeth Bristol Greenleaf entitled *Ballads and Sea Songs of Newfoundland.*

The Spirit Song of George's Bank

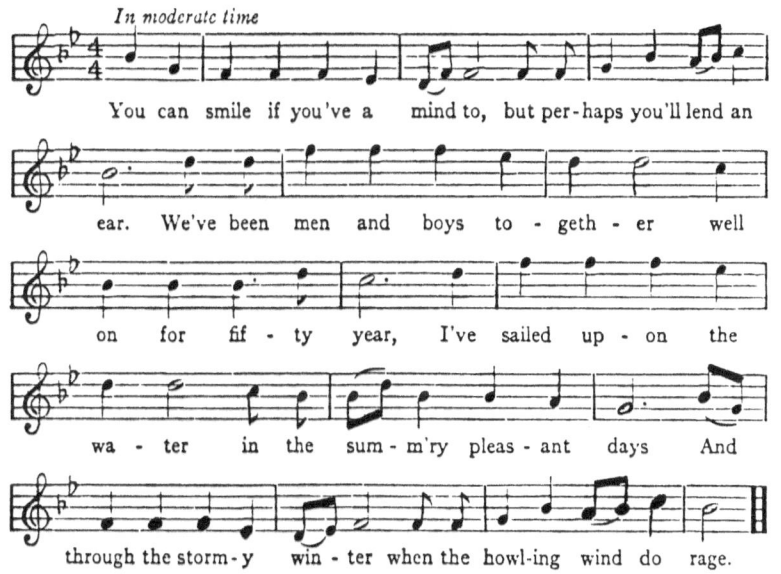

In moderate time

You can smile if you've a mind to, but per-haps you'll lend an ear. We've been men and boys to - geth - er well on for fif - ty year, I've sailed up - on the wa - ter in the sum - m'ry pleas - ant days And through the storm - y win - ter when the howl-ing wind do rage.

You can smile if you're a mind to, boys, I hope you'll lend an
ear;
We're men and boys together well on for fifty year,
Out upon the ocean, on pleasant summer days,
And when the stormy winds of winter and the howling seas do
rage.

I've been out in early seasons, most everywhere to pay:
I've been tossed about on George's, I've been fishing in the bay,
I've been out in different vessels from Western Banks to
Grand,
I've been in herring vessels that sailed down to Newfoundland.

O, not to brag myself, but I'll say nothing else but this, —
I'm not much easier frightened than most of other men,
For I've seen storms, I'll you tell, when things looked rather
blue,
But someways I was lucky, and I always did get through.

This night as I am telling you, we were off shore a ways;
I never will forget it, in all my mortal days;
I've been in our grand dog- watch, I felt a shivering dread
Came over me, as if I heard one calling from the dead.

'Twas over our rail they climbed, all silent one by one,
A dozen dripping sailors, — just wait till I am done —
Their face shone pale with seaweed, shone ghostly through the
night,
And each man took his station as if he had a right.

We moved along together there till land did heave in sight,

And rather than I should say so, the lighthouse shoned his
light,
And then those ghostly seamen moved to the rail again
And vanished in a moment before the sun of men.

We sailed right in the harbor, and every mother's son
Will tell you the same story, the same as I have done;
The trip before the other, we was on George's Bank then,
Ran down another old vessel, and sank her and all her men.

I think it was the same pore fellows — may God now rest their
souls! —
That our old craft runned over that night on George's Shoals.
So now I've told my story, to you I will confess,
I have believed in spirits from that day unto this.

(Words from Daniel Endicott)

*Daniel Endicott, his wife Fanny Jane, and their children,
Thomas and Joan were the family with whom Elisabeth Bristol
boarded while she taught school in Sally's Cove for the
International Grenfell Association in 1920. Mr. Endicott, like
many Newfoundlanders of his day, had committed literally
hundreds of songs to memory, and could sing for hours to
entertain his listeners. It is interesting to note that about the
same time that Miss Bristol was collecting this song, young
Joan Endicott was composing the words for another
Newfoundland folksong, "The Wreck of the Florizel".*

Understanding What You Have Read

1. Why does the singer give such a detailed listing of his fishing
   experience early in the song?

2. Why does he feel compelled to tell us that he is not easily frightened?

3. What explanation of the ghosts' actions is offered? Is there another explanation?

Things To Do

1. Use a good atlas or marine map to locate George's Bank.

2. Read "The Rhyme of the Ancient Mariner" by Samuel T. Coleridge. Find points of similarity and points of difference with this song.

3. Sing this song yourself, or find someone to sing it, using the music provided. Remember that the last half of the last line should be spoken, not sung.

* * *

Ben Hansen

Getting Ready To Read

Every Newfoundland community has its share of superstitions and ghost stories, often based on some event which happened in the long gone past. Many ghost stories are about ships which appear suddenly, fire guns, burst into flame, or sink slowly with all lights blazing. Sometimes they are seen by more than one person, or so we are told.

In this story Len Margaret presents a ghost story in an unusual way. The point of view is that of a young person who longs to have the experience of seeing a real ghost ship, but perhaps is not ready yet to be given that privilege. Perhaps, though, the uncle pretends to see the ship. Perhaps he wants so strongly to see her that his imagination plays tricks on him. The reader has to decide what to believe.

Every short story has a dominant element, such as the plot, or a character, or the atmosphere. In this one the dominant element is atmosphere. The other elements are only partially developed. Notice how the sounds and sights contribute to the atmosphere. See if you can spot where the atmosphere changes.

The Ghost Ship

It was a still night in August. I waited fearfully, although my uncle was with me, hoping to see the ghost ship that appeared in the Reach always about this time of year.

It was a bit scary, sitting there, in the pitch black dark with my knees hunched under my chin and my back pressed against the breakwater. I almost wished I hadn't come, but I had begged my uncle to take me here ever since Billy and his father had climbed Calvary Hill to watch the sun dance on Easter morning. I wasn't feeling a bit brave like Billy said he was. I wished I was up in the house, looking through the window at the Reach instead of here under the breakwater. Every little sound made me nervous and when a stone rolled from the cliffside, I waited for it to drop in the landwash, but it didn't. I wondered about that.

The sea was calm except for the small lops that sighed and

gurgled around the kelpy rocks on the beach and I never thought a night could be so dark. I couldn't see my uncle's face but I was able to make out the glow of the ashes on his pipe and the smell of the tobacco drifted across my face. I coughed and the sound echoed in the cliffs of the Cove. A dog barked far back in a yard and it sounded like a whole pack as the echoes bounced back from the hill. Someone slammed a door and the night was still again.

My uncle shifted his weight. "We'll soon see her now" he said and went on to tell of the times he had watched her from the jiggin' cove as if it was just the *Home* or the *Argyle* we had come here to see.

"There's her top lights now," he said. "See how she sits in the water? When she comes handier up the Reach, you'll be able to see her lower deck all lit up. She's a steamer of some kind with her flag at half-mast and there's never any smoke comin' from her funnels." He scratched a match on the tap of his boot and relit his pipe.

"Can you hear the music now?" he asked me.

The wind was beginning to rise. It swished in the crags on the hillside and made the stage door squeak on its hinges. Sea-fires glinted on the mooring ropes as the motor boats swayed on the collar.

"She looks good, all lit up like that," I said, because I didn't want to disappoint him. "Maybe grown up people are the only ones allowed to see ghost ships," I said to myself without speaking, but I'd still be able to describe her to Billy, word for word, just like my uncle had described her to me.

After a while, he tapped the tobacco from his pipe and stood up. "I have to copper my punt tomorrow," he said, "that's if it don't rain or something."

A clear spot lumed in the sky over the Red Land and the waves splashed high in the landwash.

I kept close to him as we walked up the lane and hoped for his sake he really believed that I had seen the ghost ship.

I told Billy all about her one evening just before dark, when we were sitting on the breakwater with nothing better to do.

Len Margaret

Len Margaret (a pen-name) was born in St. Leonard's, Placentia Bay. Her poetry has appeared in anthologies and literary journals and she is the author of **Fish & Brewis, Toutens & Tales** *(Canada's Atlantic Folklore/Folklife Series, no. 7).*

Understanding What You Have Read

1. This seems like a story in which a young person simply humours an old man who is imagining things. Do you see how it may be a real ghost story?

2. Can you say what might happen immediately after the end of the story?

3. What evidence is there that the uncle was not deliberately making up his story?

4. List several incidents or events which contribute to the atmosphere of apprehension.

Things To Do

1. Write an outline for a ghost story which has an unusual twist at the end.

2. Ghost stories are often based on superstition. There are many superstitions in *A Rope Against The Sun* by Al Pittman. Borrow a copy from your library and read it.

* * *

This story tells of the daring of a boy, the courage and love of a woman, and the devotion of a dog. It is easy for us to read it and pay attention only to the plot, which is indeed an exciting one. But we have to be aware of other important aspects of this short story. The atmosphere and setting convey something of what it was like to live in remote parts of Labrador during the first part of this century. The development of character, while not complete, helps us understand the difficulties of living in such an isolated region, and the importance to the family of each member. We learn from Aunt Rachel how trying it was, when all that a woman could do was to sit alone, prepare for any possibility, and wait. As you read this story, watch for the one line in her speech which sums this up.

White Fox

Uncle Ike Wilson was a born rover. In his early days he ran away from his father's farm in England, being possessed by that inborn desire of so many English lads to go to sea. It carried Uncle Ike almost all over the world, and at length it brought him to Labrador, where he thought he had found the poor man's paradise. Here was all the land he wanted, free to all comers. Here were fish in the sea and rivers, birds and bear and deer for food and furs; no taxes to pay, no social inequalities to remind him of his humble origin. Here men seemed free and equal, simple-minded, hospitable, while their livelihood depended only on their own resourcefulness.

In due time he married, though somewhat late in life, and had one son. In order to have "plenty of room," such as he needed for his trapping, he had made his winter home far up beyond the head of one of the many long inlets of the Coast; and as he was exceedingly clever at all kinds of woodcraft and animal lore, he had done remarkably well.

But it is not remarkable, as his wife was the daughter of an old settler on the Coast, that their son Jim should possess more than the usual quota of those natural abilities that go to make a valuable scout, and which we, brought up in civilization, have so often to acquire by painful and tedious work.

At the time of this story, Jim was still only fourteen years old. His hardy physical life had toughened his muscles, and already inured him to endure circumstances under which a "softy" would be about as useful as a piece of blotting-paper. From his sailor father he had learned those practical handicrafts which help out so invaluably in a tight corner. It was no trouble to him to hit the same spot twice with his axe, or tie a knot that would neither come loose nor jam.

It was the very middle of winter. The snow lay deep on the ground, and everything, everywhere, except the tops of the trees, was buried out of sight. On the barrens, wind-swept and hard-packed, the least mark on the surface might be visible for days; but in the woods the drift only left light snow many feet deep, where any mark, or even an object, became buried in a few minutes.

On the days between his long rounds over his fur-path, it was Uncle Ike's custom to go into the woods and "spell" out such firewood as was necessary to keep the stove going for his old wife.

This incident occurred on just one of these occasions. The old man had started at the first streak of dawn, as was his invariable habit, and had taken with him his team of six as stout dogs as ever helped to haul a sledge over ice. It was a glorious morning, and Jim had been allowed to go off on his little fur-round of some half-dozen traps — all his own. The price of whatever pelts he got was placed in his special stocking, that he might learn the value of things when he came to have a rifle and hunting-kit of his own.

Sundown is early in a Labrador winter, and Jim did not get home till so late that, with all his knowledge of the country, he was glad enough to see the twinkle of the light through the darkness as he sturdily trudged along the last mile homeward. For it had "turned nasty," the wind had shifted to the east, and it was snowing hard, which added greatly to the darkness of the evening. But that night Jim noticed neither weariness nor difficulty, nor did he feel the extra weight of the burden he was carrying on his back. Two days previously he had found a queer, gouged-looking mark on the snow near the "rattle," or running water, on the river that crossed his fur-path, and it was not necessary for him to look twice to see that it was the rub of a big otter. Today success had crowned his skill, and he was dragging home on his back the first otter he had ever caught by himself. What a surprise it would be for mother and father! What a good time would be his by the crackling fire, as the storm raged outside and he sat toasting his legs and telling of his adventures!

As he expected, a truly rapturous greeting awaited him, when at length he entered the door, additionally demonstrative, he thought at first, because of his large otter. Soon he found, however, it was because mother had been anxious, as neither of "her men" had returned, and now she had one wanderer anyhow.

Aunt Rachel was no longer a strong woman physically. Of late a weakness, strange altogether to her younger days, had forced her unwillingly to recognize that only by much resting between "spells" could she keep pace even with the few domestic duties which her small house made necessary.

"Get your things, Jim, and we'll have tea on the table by the time Dad comes. You can cut up a bit more wood, and we will have an extra large fire tonight. Dad'll be cold after his long day's work."

"Right you are, Mother," said the tired Jim, forgetting his aching bones in the excitement of the occasion. He was outside in a minute, axe in hand, looking for another log or two.

Now another hour had passed by. Still no sign of Uncle Ike. Everything stood ready, and the kettle was just puffing out greetings from the hob.

"Better get tea, Jim. Dad may be kept by something. But he's always home before now."

The wind was howling outside, and Aunt Rachel's face was paler than usual in spite of the firelight. Something must be wrong with Ike. The house was miles away from any neighbor, and it was utterly impossible on a night like this to seek help that way. Yet if anything had happened to her husband, he would certainly be dead before daybreak.

"What's that, Jim?" she suddenly cried out. "Surely that's a dog outside." Jim, whose ears had not been so spry just for the moment, owing to his being in the midst of his long-delayed supper, listened for a second. "That's White Fox's whine, Mother. I'd know it anywhere." And, jumping up, he ran to the door, as he supposed, to welcome his father. But no father answered his call from the darkness, only a great snow-covered furry animal that leaped up and kissed his face. "Down, Fox, down. Where's Dad?" But for answer all he got was a whine, and what he took to be an invitation to follow her, White Fox being the trusted leader of their team for three years now.

"Mother, it's White Fox all right. She's got no harness on. I'll go and see if the others are back too."

A moment later, and Jim was in from the dog pen. "They're all home but one, Mother. There's Jess and Snowball and Spry and Watch, all of them with their harnesses on, and their traces chewed through. Father must be in the woods somewhere. But where's Curly, and how did they come to leave her behind?"

The anxiety was becoming almost too much for the poor woman to bear. No help could be got from outside, and she couldn't travel fifty yards in that snow herself, with the thermometer at twenty below zero. Jim was tired and young, ever so young to go out into the dark and storm, and be of any use. She had him safe, anyhow. Surely it would only make matters worse to send him out again.

Jim had fed the dogs, and by all the laws of dogdom they should now be curled up and fast asleep in their cozy little house. But he had hardly closed the door when a scratching and the familiar whine outside said plainly that White Fox was not satisfied, and wanted something which they had failed to give her.

Again Jim went to the doorway. The bitter blast and snow drove into the porch and through it into the house. But the great woolly figure of the dog showed in the light which streamed from the cottage. As Jim looked into her eyes he could plainly understand her meaning, reading the message as well as if it were written.

"She wants me to go out with her, Mother," he called from the porch. "What shall I do? I'm almost sure she has left Father somewhere, and wants me to go and help her fetch him home."

"Shut the door and come in, Jim. I don't think I dare let you go. You and your father are all I have on earth, and if you got lost, too, I should never live through it."

There was a momentary silence, as the boy, with thoughtfulness beyond his years, stood listening.

Then once again came the familiar whine, ringing through the darkness of the night. White Fox had not given up her attempt to convey her message because she had met with two rebuffs. She knew well enough that the team would follow her if only she could persuade Jim to answer her call.

Still absolute silence reigned in the cottage. Neither mother nor son spoke. Then again came the long, piteous wail of the dog, and it seemed to the alert ears of the woman that now there was a tinge of disappointment in it.

It was she who broke the silence. "You must go, Jim. There is no help for it. That call would haunt me to my dying day if I left undone anything that could be done. Get on your things, boy. Take your father's lantern, and God help you. I shan't have long to wait anyhow, without you two, if you never come back again."

Jim was already half into his oilskin suit, his storm-cap, skin mitts, and moccasins, while his mother packed up a few things which might be necessary in case an accident had happened. Indeed, he was already moving to the door when she called him back again. "Jim," she said, "kiss me once more. It may be the last time I'll ever see you alive. And then we'll just kneel down and ask God, who loves you better than I can, to be with you tonight and bring you safe back with Father."

At last the door had closed behind him, and, marvel of marvels, Aunt Rachel, weary and exhausted, fell asleep in her chair, and in the God-given rest was able to economize her store of strength to meet the ordeal she had yet to go through.

Jim meanwhile had found a spare harness, and put it on White Fox, tying the trace around his waist. Then he called out the rest of the team, tying their traces together and hitching them on his arm. Since he had no idea of where he was going, there was only one thing he could do, and that was to follow the dog. So, closing his eyes, as seeing was out of the question, and they were safer anyhow that way from twigs and branches after they got among the woods, he ploughed his way as rapidly as he could, following all the time the tugging of White Fox's trace by keeping his right hand on the line.

Fortunately for all concerned, the spot of woods which Uncle Ike had selected for his winter's cutting was less than two miles from the house, and of that one mile was over a frozen lake, where, although the full blast of the storm made the cold more bitter and harder to stem, yet the drift was packed or altogether cleared away by the violence of the wind. Through the drogues* of woods in the narrow gulches the young snow was so soft that the boy had almost to swim, and but for the tug, tug, of White Fox's trace he could never for an instant have kept his direction, or even made progress. But White Fox scaled nearly a hundred pounds, and stood twenty-seven inches to the shoulder, and was actually heavier than the boy himself; while every ounce of her was made up of bone and iron muscles.

One other element told strongly in the boy's favor and enabled him to accomplish what must otherwise have been an almost impossible task. It never entered his head that the dog could be mistaken. He trusted White Fox as implicitly as he would his mother. Of course his chum knew better than any one else on earth what to do, and if he could only last out and do his part, he knew well it was a mere piece of child's play to the dog.

Once and again, as he floundered through a deeper drift than usual, he became completely stalled, and it seemed impossible ever to extricate himself. He was nearly played out, and the cold and dark made the temptation to rest just for a minute almost irresistible. The excitement of the first hour had enabled him to call into play at once all his reserve strength, but now he felt he must sleep — only a moment, of course, but just a minute's nap. In those deep drifts, not even White Fox could have hauled so heavy a load. All she could do was to employ her powers of suggestion. She returned to her lagging master, and kissed his face, incidentally running to and fro and hardening a path for him on which he could crawl out of the bog of snow.

Once more they ploughed along on their way. Scarcely a sound was audible; just the moaning of the storm, and now and again a rare whimper or snarl from one of the dogs as one of the others got in his road. Indeed, the silence and darkness were almost visible. Suddenly, quite close at hand, a dog's call resounded from the bush, and White Fox leaped in the direction with such violence as to fling the boy clean off his feet, rolling him over once more in the deep snow.

But that he no longer noticed: it was Curly's sharp bark. Picking himself up, and bracing himself for the effort, Jim shouted with all his might. "Father! Father! Father!" But the only answer was a howl in unison from all the dogs, and the soughing of the storm through the firs and spruces of the grove they had entered.

Only for a moment, however, was there any doubt what to do; and again it was White Fox who brought the solution. For she hauled off into the bush at the side of the path, and began burrowing down into the snow. Jim followed, not without a sinking feeling at heart, and in less than a minute was kneeling over the prostrate body of his father.

"Father! Father! It's me — Jim." But no answer still. Yes, he was breathing, breathing loudly. And warm, too, where Curly had evidently been cuddled up against him. There was only one chance. Could he find the wood sledge? For if so he might be able to save his father's life.

Curly was bubbling over with joy, and probably connecting Jim's arrival with the chance for some supper after all. She was dancing all about, entangling her trace around Jim's legs, and positively forcing him to notice it. Seizing it with his hands, he followed it along. It seemed never to end, though really it was only thirty feet long, but it was entangled again and again in the bushes, and over it all the deep snow had fallen. He had guessed that the dog was still fast to the sledge, and so he found it at last, the sharp upturned prow of the komatik jabbing right into his hand from the drift as he groped after it in the dark.

It must have taken another full hour to dig the sledge out, and haul it alongside Uncle Ike, to drag the limp and helpless body upon it, and then so to fix it with lashings that his father could not fall off on the journey home.

A team of dogs going home on a night of that kind is almost as irresistible as a traction engine, and Jim's only trouble was to keep the sledge right side up. That he somehow succeeded is actually certain, for in the early hours of the morning, Aunt Rachel was roused by the sound of the dogs outside.

It was now her chance to call on her reserve strength, and that she certainly must have done. Buoyed up by his success, Jim's endurance did not fail him either, and, guided by the intuitive knowledge of a good housewife, the two were soon chafing Uncle Ike's half-frozen limbs, as he lay before a gorgeous fire, rolled in warm Hudson's Bay "four-point" blankets.

It was not long before a little hot nourishment was successfully forced between his lips, and he was able to open his eyes and give the anxious watchers a smile of recognition.

Uncle Ike was never quite able to remember how it all happened. He had reached the clump, tied up his team, and was cutting away, when suddenly he felt odd, dropped his axe, and could no longer stand upright. However, he had sufficient mental power left to reason that his only chance lay in reaching his sledge. The dogs instantly answered his call, but they were all fast to the komatik and were unable to reach him, as that was purposely tied to a stump. That was all he knew, except that one dog at last got near him as he lay, and cuddling up close to him, kept him from freezing to death. The others in their excitement had chewed through their traces or, as White Fox had done, succeeded in slipping their harnesses.

Then White Fox must have hurried home for help, and the other dogs that could get loose had followed her — as they were always used to doing.

No, White Fox was not forgotten. Jim says before he lay down to sleep he could not help just going out to give Curly some supper, and a few extra little titbits for White Fox, but he found her as peacefully asleep as if she had done nothing unusual. She slept that night as many a "better-off" being has never known how.

Wilfred Thomason Grenfell

Wilfred Grenfell was an English doctor and missionary who came to Labrador around the turn of the century to care for the spiritual and medical needs of the fishermen who lived there. His activities in Northern Newfoundland and in Labrador are legendary. His beneficial effect on the lives of the people was immense, and the result of his work is still with us in the form of the hospitals and services of the International Grenfell Association.

Many of Dr. Grenfell's books were written to raise money for his mission in Newfoundland, but we can assume were also written to satisfy Dr. Grenfell's desire to make the character and circumstances of these Northern Newfoundland people known to the world.

Understanding What You Have Read

1. Courage is one theme in this story. Who displays greatest courage? Support your answer.

2. Write a full description of White Fox.

3. What things combined to help Jim find his father?

4. Rewrite part of the story from Aunt Rachel's point of view.

5. Dr. Grenfell was a missionary as well as a doctor. Can you find evidence of this in this story?

Things To Do

1. White Fox was a leader. Find out as much as you can about Labrador dog teams and what being leader meant.

2. Invent another set of circumstances to explain Ike's being in trouble in the woods.

3. To get a better idea of life in Labrador in those days read *Woman of Labrador* by Elizabeth Goudie.

* * *

Getting Ready to Read

If you have ever felt left on your own with nobody to help you, comfort you or keep you company, you have experienced just a little of the sadness of the speaker, Victor Butler. Mr. Butler believes that one of the greatest tragedies in his life was caused by the setting in which he lived. The setting for the following autobiography is the Newfoundland outport of Harbour Buffett in the 1930s. But how could the setting cause a tragedy? You must realize that the setting in a story includes the time and place of action. Time and place influence people's attitudes and actions. It is the people's attitudes and actions that cause Mr. Butler to say that people, in times of trouble, can be precious small help.

Willie

I was working all the time when July came and tragedy struck my family. My two boys caught a severe cold and had to stay away from school. The older boy, Sam, recovered after a few days. The younger boy, Willie, did not improve. He became listless and lay around the house.

We still thought it was a severe cold that would wear away eventually. He did not improve and we became very concerned. There was no medical officer in the Harbour to advise us as to the cause of the trouble. We were not aware how serious his condition was. I was very worried as I did not have any money to hire a boat to take him to Argentia Cottage Hospital. This was a very serious matter and very disturbing; there was nothing I could do about it.

I had to get the boy to hospital by some means. There was a constable stationed in the Harbour at the time and a clergyman as well. My associates owned boats but none raised a helping hand to try and save a young boy's life. I borrowed an open boat with a five horse power Hubbard motor from John Collett, a man operating a small business in the north west of the Harbour. He was a very sympathetic man. He only charged me fifty cents for the gas.

Next morning, I took a small bed and plenty of bedding and rolled the sick boy in the clothes on board the boat. There was a covered part at the bow, enough to shelter him from getting wet. I left for Argentia. My son Sam went with me. He was eleven years old; the sick boy, Willie, was nine.

The distance to Argentia from Buffett is eighteen miles. When we were half way to Argentia, the wind began to blow from the southwest. We were getting a lot of water over the boat. I had to cover Sam with a piece of canvas behind the engine box to keep him dry. It took four and a half hours to reach Argentia. I carried Willie the half mile to the hospital in my arms as I had no money to pay transportation costs.

The doctor pronounced that the boy had meningitis* and there was not much hope for his recovery.

There was too much wind to return home to Buffett. I had no means to moor the boat safely, so I had to beach her.

We had only a small lunch with us. I had a few cents with me; I bought some biscuits and a small piece of cheese. We had to stay in the boat all night. I made Sam crawl into the shelter of the forward deck and covered him with bedding. I put on my oilskins, and lay down in the bottom of the boat.

During the night the wind veered from southeast and blew a gale with rain. The tide was rising. As soon as the boat floated, I had to take her out of the beach to save her from being wrecked. It was blowing white smokes of wind. I managed to steam across to Salmonier on the opposite side of Argentia. There was a jack boat anchored there with a man and boy on board. The man let Sam stay on board with very poor grace. I did not mind myself so much. I was afraid Sam would catch cold. After giving him the few biscuits and small piece of cheese, I had nothing to eat myself.

I had to take the boat under the land and tie up at a man's wharf. It was still raining, so I rolled in the canvas* and lay in the bottom of the boat. I was so used to hardship I took reverses as a matter of course. The man gave Sam a cup of tea. They were living on dole. The wind moderated and we came home next day.

Willie lived a week. One morning I received a telegram saying he had died. I made a coffin that day and in the late evening I borrowed Mr. Collett's boat. My cousin, Leslie Butler, went with me.

We had a bad time on the way to Argentia. It was nightfall when we left Buffett. The fog was thick, a strong breeze was blowing from southwest and there was a big swell in the water. I had to use a flashlight to see the compass. This proved very awkward as I had to hold the compass with one hand to keep it from washing overboard with the sea breaking over the bow of the boat. This meant that I had to steer with one hand and could only glance at the compass occasionally.

When we made the land near Hole in Wall Island we were a bit off course. We were among the Follock rocks and sunkers* were breaking mountains high all around us. Being used to sailing around the Bay so much I knew where we were and did not get wrecked.

At 11:00 p.m. we arrived at the hospital. We put the corpse in the coffin. I took the coffin on my shoulder and brought it to the boat. We lay down until daylight and came home.

All this was a severe trial for me and my wife. For her it was almost unbearable, as she was pregnant at the time and this added to her worries.

No one will ever know the effect the death of my boy had on me. Besides mourning the boy's death I felt bad about the way he died without my being in a position to get medical aid in time to give him a chance to live, for want of twenty dollars to hire a boat and get him to hospital in time.

I always kept my troubles to myself and never let my emotions show. I became morose* and just about lost confidence in human nature, especially my associates and the clergy particularly as I did not get any help from anyone in my time of need. All this caused me to have a different outlook on life. From this experience, I learned a lesson that I'll never forget — if a man is not self-sufficient, what help he will get from others will be small.

When I commenced to write this record of the Depression years — some of the sad events of that time seemed as a hazy memory of a half-forgotten dream. Sometimes I feel sorry I have written on those events, as writing them in detail has renewed the clear picture of hardship, suffering and tragedy that I had almost forgotten.

Victor Butler

Victor Butler is a nineteenth century Newfoundlandler who was born on March 29th, 1896, at Harbour Buffett, Placentia Bay. Having worked all his life as general "jack-of-all-trades" in that community, he moved to Arnold's Cove, Placentia Bay in 1967 where he continues to fish and build boats.

Understanding What You Have Read

1. As a result of this tragic experience, Victor Butler writes — "if a man is not self-sufficient what help he will get from others will be small."

   a) What does self-sufficient mean?
   b) Was Victor Butler completely self-sufficient in coping with his son's illness?
   c) From your own experiences do you think that this statement is correct?

2. Was Willie as much a victim of his environment as he was of meningitis?

3. What effect has writing about his son's death had on Mr. Butler?

Things To Do

1. Write a short autobiographical account in which you relate a memorable experience in your life.

2. If you enjoyed "Willie" you will probably enjoy the book from which it was taken, *S'posin' I Dies In The Dory.*

Ben Hansen

FOREBEARS

PART II

Cut Deep In Marble

In this section we are concerned with the effects of extreme physical and intellectual isolation. Norman Duncan suggests the effects on children and the breaking strain it could place on parents. Ron Pollett and Grace Butt present two different characters for our study; 'Peter' lives cunningly, taking intelligent advantage of every break he can get, 'Mrs. Kollin' lives by honest and honorable toil. Georgiana Cooper's people are sturdy, fearless, kind and cheerful. They have names cut deep in marble although the physical evidence of their lives has all but disappeared. Finally Paul O'Neill reminds us that many of our forebears took up arms to defend their values, but that the victory of violence brings no celebration to our peaceful land.

Ben Hansen

Getting Ready To Read

Strictly speaking, an outport in Newfoundland is any community outside of St. John's, or, at least, that was the surface meaning of the word, but it really meant more than that. Right up to the last twenty years or so the term outport suggested, especially to non-Newfoundlanders, a small fishing village that had little or no contact with the outside world.

These excerpts from "Newfoundlanders of the Outports," written by Norman Duncan, and first published in 1901, relate two typical experiences in the lives of outport Newfoundlanders until recent times. Both incidents deal with children. As you read try to determine the worst effects on children of the absence of teachers, doctors and clergy.

The Outports

We were seated on the Head, high above the sea, watching the fleet of punts come from the Mad Mull grounds and from the nets along shore, for it was evening. Jack, my young friend, had told me much of the lore* of lobster-catching and squid-jigging. Of winds and tides and long breakers he had given me solemn warnings — especially of that little valley down which the gusts came, no man knew from where. He had imparted certain secrets concerning the whereabouts of gulls' nests and juniper-berry patches, for I had won his confidence. I had been informed that Uncle Tom Bull's punt was in hourly danger of turning over because her spread of canvas was "scandalous" great, that Bill Bludgett kept the "surliest dog in the Harbor," that the "goats was wonderful hard t'find" in the fog, that a brass bracelet would cure salt-water sores on the wrists, that — I cannot recall it all. He had "mocked" a goat, a squid, a lamb, old George Walker at prayer, and "Aunt" Ruth berating "Uncle" Simon for leaving the splitting table unclean....

He asked me riddles, thence he passed to other questions, for he was a boy who wondered, and wondered, what lay beyond those places which he could see from the highest hill. I described a street and a pavement, told him that the earth was round, defined a team of horses, corrected his impression that a church organ was played with the mouth and denied the reports that the flakes and stages of New York were the largest in the world. The boys of the outports do not play games — there is no time, and at any rate, the old West Country games have not come down to this generation with the dialect, so I told him how to play tag, hide-and-seek and blind-man's buff, and proved to him that they might be interesting, though I had to admit they might not be profitable in certain cases.

"Some men," said I, at last, "have never seen the sea."

He looked at me and laughed his unbelief. "Sure," said he, "not a hundred haven't?"

"Many more than that."

" 'Tis hard t' believe, zur," he said. "Terrible hard."

We were silent while he thought it over.

"What's the last harbor in the world?" he asked.

I hesitated.

"The very last, zur! They do say 'tis St. John's. But, sure, zur, they must be something beyond. What do it be?" After a silence he continued, speaking wistfully, "What's the last harbor in all the world, zur? Doesn't you know?"

† † † † †

The hills overhang Little Harbor and the sea grimly confronts it. It was settled from Greater Harbor when the crowd of souls there — five hundred all told — became too great for some men longer to bear with. The thirty cottages grip the rocks for dear life. All the men are fisher folk. They are far remote from their kind. There are no roads on the northeast coast. All the world's a waste.

When we stepped ashore, an old fisherman with seven children tagging after him came down to greet us.

"Good even, zur."

"Good evening."

"Be you a doctor?"

"No, sir."

"Noa? Isn't you? Now, I thought maybe you might be." Disappointment first showed in his voice when he said, "But you isn't, you says."

"Sorry — but no."

"Sure, I thought you might be a doctor. They be great need of a doctor on this coast, zur. Sure, the nearest do be at Tilt Cove an' tis sixty miles away. We do be too poor t'send for un. But you isn't a doctor, you say? Is you sure, zur?"

He looked at me wistfully, half doubtingly. He waited for me to answer.

"I thought you might be," he went on. "Perhaps you might know something about doctorin'. Noa?"

"Nothing."

"I thought now, that you might. 'Tis my little girl what's sick. Sure, none of us knows what do be the matter with she. Woan't you come up an' see she, zur? Perhaps you might do something — though — you isn't — a doctor."

The little girl was lying on the floor — on a ragged quilt, in a corner. She was covered to her chin, and the covering quivered now and again, as though she were shaken with cold. She was a fair child — a little girl of seven. Her eyes were deep blue, wide and fringed with long, heavy lashes. Her hair was flaxen, abundant and all curly and tangled. She was so winsome and lovely!

"I thinks she do be goain' t'die soon," said the mother. " 'Tis queer. She do be all swelled in the legs. Sure, she can't stand. We been waitin' for a doctor t'come, an' we thought perhaps you was one."

"How long have you waited?"

" 'Twas in April she was took. She've been lyin' there ever since. 'Tis near August now, I'm thinkin'. We've been waitin' — sort of expectin' a doctor would come. They was one here 'bout two years ago."

"Think they'll be one comin' soon?" said the old man.

I took the little girl's hand. It was dry and hot. She looked in my face — but I could not interpret. She did not smile — nor did she fear me. Her fingers closed over mine. I do not know what she meant by that tight clasp. She was a beautiful child, a blue-eyed, winsome little thing; but pain had driven all the sweet roguery out of her face.

"Does you think she'll die, zur?" asked the woman, anxiously.

I did not know.

"Sure, zur," said the man, trying to smile, "I thought you might be a doctor when — I seed you — comin' ashoare."

"But you isn't?" said the woman. "Is you sure you couldn't do anything? Be you noa kind of a doctor at all? We doan't — we doan't — want she t'die."

In the silence — so long and deep a silence — melancholy shadows crept in from the desolation without.

"I wish you was a doctor," said the man. "I wish you — was." He was crying.

Norman Duncan

Norman Duncan (1871-1916) was born in Brantford, Ontario. During the summer of 1900 he visited the Exploits area of Notre Dame Bay and quickly became entranced by the environment and the people he found there. For five or more consecutive years he returned to Newfoundland to spend his summers, delighting in his surroundings and coming to respect and admire the people he lived among. These summer experiences provided the material and inspiration for his numerous short stories, essays and novels set in Newfoundland. He published **The Way of the Sea** *(1903),* **Dr. Luke of the Labrador** *(1904),* **Dr. Grenfell's Parish** *(1905) and* **The Cruise of The Shining Light** *(1907). He is best known by younger readers for his two collections of short stories* **The Adventures of Billy Topsail** *and* **Billy Topsail and Company.**

Understanding What You Have Read

1. In age, Jack is a boy. In what ways is he not a boy?

2. Which of the following describe Jack? Dull, ignorant, stunned (stupid), curious, interesting, knowledgeable,

inventive. Support each choice by reference to the story.

3. The fact that more than hundreds of men have not seen the sea, and that the farthest harbour in the world was not St. John's, amaze Jack. Do those facts amaze you? What, then, is the major difference, between you and Jack? What is responsible for this difference? Does this make you better than Jack?

4. How does the writer make the coming death of the girl so sad and tragic? Why will the girl die? How do we know she is going to die?

Things To Do

1. Many words we use in our writing and everyday speech have denotations and connotations. Denotations are the strict, obvious meanings of words: connotations are ideas or images we associate or think of when we read or hear certain words. For example, the denotations of black are dark, and absence of light, but the connotations are evil, fear, ignorance, blindness. Fire has as a denotation the flame caused by burning, but its connotations are warmth, desire, curiosity, life. Give as many connotations as you can think of for the following: blue; white; rainbow; eagle; youth; isolation; death.

2. For a more lighthearted, romantic picture of life in a Newfoundland outport read *Tales From Pigeon Inlet* by Ted Russell.

* * *

Getting Ready To Read

"Everyone who has lived in an outport knows a character like Peter the Grate. He's always going some place or coming back.... He seldom works at a set job — never punched a time clock in his life — and for him every day's a holiday. Yet he gets along as well as everyone else." So wrote Ron Pollett in his introduction to his character study of Peter the Grate, and so he suggests that all of us, at times, would like to be a Peter the Grate.

"Peter the Grate" is a biography — an account of someone's life. In reading this excerpt from Peter the Grate, concern yourself with more than the things Peter said and did. The real value of reading a biography is to come to appreciate why a person acts in certain ways, and thereby judge our own actions. Ask yourself was Peter happy or unhappy? Should he have been pitied, scorned or loved? Do we all have some of Peter's ways?

Peter The Grate

All I can say is, it's a darn shame he had to go and die so soon after getting the money. Here he was, on the pig's back for the first time in all his eighty years, and he had to go right away and kick the bucket.

I'm talking about Peter the Grate, that half-baked character who lived and died in our place in the bottom of Trinity Bay. That is, a lot of people said he was half-baked. But I never thought so. He was a sort of friend of mine. He was only a bit strange. I like unusual people if they're as funny as Peter. Peter made a lot of laughs in his day.

Peter was an only son and in my early days lived with his parents. Their old house — the oldest in the harbor, I guess, the way it looked — was on the hillside near the bridge. The bridge was the meeting place for all the summer loafers and roadside sitters in the evenings just before dark and also the spot where we schoolboys spent our off-hours trouting over the rail. All day and far into the night, rain or shine, from spring till fall, Peter was on that bridge — trouting, eeling, gabbing, or just sitting on the handstay. He went home only long enough to bolt his meals and snatch a wink of sleep.

His only complaint was that his hands and feet were always cold. He wore three pairs of socks all the time and two pairs of cuffs in winter. Even at that he kept stomping his feet and beating his hands together as soon as the weather got a bit nippy. On frosty days his lips turned blue and his teeth chattered and he got the shakes the way some people do in swimming. Someone joked that Peter had cold blood in his veins like the fish, or maybe only cold water.

His father had a carpenter shop alongside the house where he turned out table legs, window and door sashes, and bannisters. The old man invented all sorts of contraptions, rigged with pedals and levers to make his work easier and carpenters from all over dropped in to watch and admire. But Peter never bothered with the interesting shop although there was a bit of ready cash in the business — never helped his father turn a hand and never learned how to do anything.

All he did was loaf around the bridge or wherever else he might find company and fun. For, as I said before, Peter liked to be among crowds. He was in his glee listening to a bunch of people batting the breeze, no matter what they were prating* about. And his big ears spread like mainsails to every whiff of gossip as his gimlet* eyes prodded about among the faces chewing the rag.

After his parents died, he used up everything around the shop for firewood. Cutting and hauling wood from the nearby drokes* was too much like work for Peter. Gradually the shop itself went into the stove, as did the fences around the yard and finally over the years his fish stage and flake.

Last off, he wore all the socks he could get into his boots and was said to wrap brin bags around his feet in bed. All fall, winter and early spring he clung around the big potbellied stove in the corner shop until closing time, then sat in the kitchen of the neighbor's house — the one who found him dead — until the fire went out for the night.

Peter lived with his guns and shot at everything except crows. He considered crows bad luck. But he had it in for the harmless seagulls, which were wild and flighty as game ducks in our section. He ate the greasy, tough old saddlebacks as well as the tender-fleshed young birds. Also, he was one of the few who trapped gulls cruelly on glides.

He always had glides on the harbor. That is, he anchored a squid or herring concealing barbs imbedded in cork which hooked into the beak or gullet of the foraging birds. If he happened to be out of the village — in the ponds trouting or otherwise busy out of sight — the gull was left to suffer a whole day before collapsing from exhaustion trying to shake the hooks. Some of the men bawled him out about that, but to no avail.

Also, every summer he robbed the gull's nests in the ponds and kept a pen full of fledglings which he gobbled up when they grew enough flesh to sink his teeth into. In the turr and bullbird season his gun was hot and his rodney bloodstained every day the weather was clear enough to take sight.

But his greatest triumph was the wild geese. These were prize birds in any hunter's language, not only because they were extremely scarce in our place but also because it took a top expert to get a shot at one. But Peter often took the harbor's breath away by popping up with not one, but two or three, slung over his shoulder.

It was some years before Peter revealed how he did it. It was so simple that only he could be expected to think it up. He found the feeding grounds miles into the wilderness on a marshy plateau and built a blind in the center. But that proved no good, because the wily geese shied off from the unfamiliar hump on the level marsh. Then he got another idea — the right one. He dug a pit and pulled camouflage overhead so the place looked untouched. Then he crouched in the hole and waited for the birds to come and feed in the evening dusk.

Once he brought out a big live gander with a wounded wing which he gave to the minister to go along with the lone domestic goose at the parsonage. The wing healed and the bird seemed at home for a spell, though nothing happened ganderwise — much to Peter's disappointment as he wanted to see what kind of "little gooses" he might get. After a year or so, one Sunday the wild bird floundered out and pitched in the harbor right before the unbelieving eyes of a devout old vestryman* coming home from Holy Communion. Sunday or not, the old fellow couldn't control his urge to bag a prize goose and ran for his gun. He pointed point blank and pulled the trigger — and nothing happened. The bird flapped out of range.

Later that day when someone told him it was the parson's gander, he nearly keeled over. "Praise be," he exclaimed. "It was Sunday and I only cracked the cap."

Peter, too, observed the Sabbath, in deference to strict custom. That is, he never shot a gun or baited a hook. But it was easy to see that temptation was jiggling his elbow all through the day because he stood on the bank watching the big trout breaching all over the tongue and he went out along shore to inspect his nets from the beach — right after coming from church in the morning! In this way he was kept so much on edge waiting for Monday he couldn't sleep on Sunday nights, it was said.

I know, when as a boy I was handlining and trawling with my father and had to start off early on Mondays to look for bait, we often passed Peter sculling his rodney about the harbor at two o'clock in the morning, three hours before daylight. It wasn't as though he was bound for the far grounds as we were, because Peter was never known to venture beyond the shelter of the headlands and indeed, only moved out of the inside harbor at all when the sea was stark calm. In this respect, there was a well-established saying about him in our place: "For rain, watch the goats; for wind, watch Peter."

It was also joked that if Peter ever set out a cod trawl it would have to be so near the beach that people would have to bar their cats in to keep them from getting tangled up in the hooks.

So the only reason Peter was out on the harbor that early on Mondays was, he was simply too impatient to wait ashore for daylight after one whole day stranded on the beach.

Although he didn't go far from home, either on water or on land, Peter was always seeing big, odd, strange, wonderful things and bragging about his adventures to anyone willing to listen. Hardly a day passed but he reported a highly unusual sight or happening. He was forever breathing marvels and spitting wonders, as someone once remarked — though in less delicate words.

"What I seen up there in the Pig's Hole in the brook this mornin'!" he would begin, stopping abruptly to squirt tobacco spit. He had a habit of punctuating his talk with tobacco squirts. Also, he jerked his head sideways violently to emphasize a point, as a lot of people did in our village, only Peter almost broke his neck doing it. He was continually blinking, too, and twitching his eyebrows and pulling at his moustache and gesturing with his hands. The only thing, he couldn't wiggle his ears. Someone said that if Peter had a tail it would never stop wagging.

"So I slung out me line in the Pig's Hole and this big salmon grabbed it. I thought sure I had holt of the breeder. But what should it turn out to be but one of those big conger eels. All I seen was his head with the long hair on it. He let out one unmerciful screech and I dropped the pole and runned. Next thing I seen was me pole towin' across the pond to the deep hole and it sunk there like a rock." You'd almost believe him, the way he told it.

"But fish don't screech, Peter," someone would inject.

Peter would bore his gimlet eyes into the doubting Thomas. "Have you ever seen a conger eel?"

Peter was on safe ground here, and he knew it. Conger eels are classed with sea monsters, of course. There was talk of them in the deep-water ponds, but it was all talk. Actually, though, fish or mammals of the monster type that make a stir in the newspapers did turn up in our section, tangled in the codtraps. Among these was the giant octopus, and Peter concocted many fanciful tales about lively encounters with these. Once when he heard of a monster shark attacking a punt and biting a chunk out of the gunwale, which actually happened, he showed up next day with marks on his own boat he said were made by a shark.

In short, he told so many lies about his adventures with strange fish, that if he had the truth to tell, no one would believe him.

He had a sharp eye for insect life, too, and made wonders about the antics of water hoppers on the brooks and forkytails in wells. He captured the large English butterfly, a rare and elusive species, and brought it to the bridge in a paper bag to show to us cluster of pop-eyed boys. And if he was in the mood, he could always give a concert of bird calls and animal noises if someone asked him to — and someone usually did. He could beat anybody at grunting like a pig.

Also, he liked to brag about his dreams, especially the one in which he met the red-and-white horse with the black star on its forehead.

"I was comin' along the mish path and this big horse was croppin' grass by the roadside. He looked up at me and said as plain as day, 'Peter, I'm Old Bob Cranford's horse and me name is Barney.' Well, sir, I knowed Old Bob was dead years before I was borned, so the first thing in the mornin' I asked me old man. Me old man says yes, Bob did have a big red-and-white horse with a black star in the forehead named Barney. And I swear I never knowed it before."

One thing that disturbed Peter was any odd sound out of the stilly night, and I think he slept with his ears open. We discovered that when one of the practical jokers rigged up a strange noise to scare Peter as the clock struck twelve. We hatched the idea when we stumbled upon a length of heavy chain left on a boat mooring up pond from the hut. We lugged the chain to camp and strung it out on some jagged rocks in a brook near the door and attached a string leading into a bunk.

That night the falltime woods was as dark and silent as a cellar. No sooner had Peter hit the sack and got snoring good than the ghost started coming. But loud!

First, the snoring stopped. Then Peter popped up like a jumping jack. Then he lit the lantern at his elbow. At that, we all sat up too, making a fuss at yawning and rubbing our eyes, and asked him what the blue blazes was the matter now he had to light the light.

He didn't answer right away, only sat there with his big ears cocked. He often stuttered when excited, and now he had to wait for the words.

"T-t-t-tender good heavens, w-w-w-what was that?" He looked around, evidently for the two dogs, which were right there on the floor standing now with their ears cocked also. One of them went to the closed door and scratched at the latch.

"What was what?" we wanted to know. "What's all this crazy stuff about, anyhow?"

"That's a queer yarn," said Peter, scratching his head. "I thought sure I heard a chain rattle. Might be an otter draggin' one of Martin Migdon's traps. Let me get the gun — I can see his eyes in the dark."

"Otter? Traps?" one fellow laughed. "Nobody got traps out yet....Sure you're not crazy in the head, Peter?"

"Yah, he must be dreamin'," the string-puller agreed. Then to Peter: "The trouble is you eat too many salt tomcods. All you heard was your stomach rattlin'."

Peter pondered that a spell, shaking his head. Then he doused the light. But no sooner had he settled back than the chain started again. He bounced up, then lay down, his bunk squeaking; but he said nothing. There was no snoring for a long time after. In the morning when he went to the brook to fill the kettles he came across the chain.

After that, he was wary of us and our shenanigans. We tried to trick him into shooting at a rabbit skin we rigged up near the camp door that was so life-like with the head and ears sticking out over a windfall we almost fooled ourselves. But Peter took one glance and said, "Boys, there never was a live rabbit yet with dead ears. Ya got a lot to learn about rabbits."

We never had to ask Peter twice to go camping with us overnight, or trouting all day, or to go any place where we had to boil the kettle. He knew we always carried plenty of sweet cake and caraway seed biscuits and excursion bread. Peter had a hungry sweet tooth — always did have — and would make a meal of crumbly currant buns and fatpork toutens and hot-oven things like that. He would follow anyone anywhere to get chocolate men and Jerusalems and bulls' eyes and sen-sens — the way boys trailed the village merchant to pick up his snipes. He drooled out of both sides of his mouth at the sight of candy, especially chewy caramels, in the shop windows, and with him an all-day sucker lasted but a minute.

Peter did pretty well with the sweets while he had his mother to give him money, because he kicked up such a fuss she had to give it to him. But now he was as poor as Job's turkey.

At age seventy-five, he started getting six dollars a month

from the government — and wood cost eight dollars a hundred sticks and coal was out of the question. Still, for some reason no one could fathom, he never touched the old sheep's house first or last to put in the stove. The neighbors took up a collection of food for him every fall, now that they had it to give, and he weathered the winters on that and the six dollars until he could fudge for himself again in the summer. He complained he couldn't keep anything on his stomach unless he had a bit of tobacco to chew in between, and the neighbors threw in a couple of plugs of Beaver, too.

He struggled along like that until Confederation, in the spring of 1949. Now he was entitled to thirty dollars monthly pension (later upped to forty) under the social security. But the pension money had to be left to pile up until the red tape was untangled, so when it finally did come in the fall Peter got a cheque for $180.

He spent eighty dollars for wood and coal and changed the rest into dollar bills which he carried in a big lump in his back pocket. He sat on it by day and slept on it at night, waiting for the first of next month to get another thirty dollars which he intended to spend for food. He asked every other person he met what date it was and how many more days till December.

The cheque came the day of his funeral.

So now he lies on a hillside facing the salt water with the woods in back. The salmon and herring breach in front of him and the gulls fly over him and the rabbits tramp on his grave. A "cow's tobacco" plant waves tall at his head, and a small spruce full of buds spreads at his feet, and the long weeds lie flat in winter to keep him warm.

Maybe Peter the Grate didn't do much good in the world. Then again, he did no great harm. The cemeteries everywhere are full of people about whom can be said the same thing.

Ron Pollett

Ron Pollett was born in New Harbour, Trinity Bay in 1900. He was a printer by trade but also did some teaching. Mr. Pollett immigrated to the U.S., where he worked as a printer until his death in 1955. He used outport subjects in his works: **The Ocean At My Door** *and* **Peter The Grate**. *Some of his stories were published in "The Atlantic Guardian."*

Understanding What You Have Read

1. To make his writing more lively and descriptive Pollett makes use of similes such as "as dark and silent as a cellar". How many other similes can you find in the story? Which ones are new and interesting, and which are old and common? Write an original simile.

2. a) What was unique about the way Peter lived his life?
   b) Was Peter stupid or shrewd? Refer to incidents in the story to support your position.

3. Does Peter remind you of any other characters you have read about this year? In what ways?

Things To Do

1. Read the complete character study of Peter in *The Ocean At My Door* by Ron Pollett.

2. Read about other interesting characters in "The Time Skipper Joe Knocked Off Swearing" by Grace Butt, and "Farley Mowat — The Fellow From Upalong" by Ray Guy. Both are in *Baffles of Wind and Tide*.

3. Pollett, in his story, "Peter the Grate," uses many interesting phrases that require you to interpret their meanings. One such phrase is "on the pig's back" which means to be enjoying one's luck or prosperity. Explain what each of the following phrases from "Peter the Grate" means:

   half-baked
   kept on edge
   red tape was untangled
   breathing marvels and spitting wonders
   doubting Thomas
   gimlet eyes

* * *

Getting Ready To Read

Some of us regard life as a chore — at best, a necessary routine. Sometimes it takes a simple down-to-earth person to make us see that one of life's lessons is to learn to take it as it is — "not docilely accepting it . . .but partaking of it." This narrative essay contains a moral for us all; that is, it has a practical meaning for its readers. Think about Mrs. Kollin as you read about her and try to say why she made such an impression on the author.

Mrs. Kollin

Know what I was doing today? — scrubbing floors. . .just the floor of my tiny kitchen area, and the even smaller area of the bathroom. They were stained, and I felt there was nothing for it but to skip the sponge mop, and get down on my knees and scrub. . . .

It made me think of old Mrs. Kollin. Did I ever tell you about Mrs. Kollin?

She used to come and help clean up my mother's house — for years and years she came.

That was before I was married. I worked in an office, and I was young and idealistic and I could get quite emotional about the difference between those who were poor and had to work hard and those who were well off and didn't (or so it seemed to me). I used to think that the pain you can get in your back from being tensed up over a typewriter all day was different from the pain you get from bending over a scrubbing bucket.

I remember sometimes when I'd get home and find Mrs. Kollin down on her knees cleaning up the front porch all my end-of-the-day pleasure would evaporate. I would say Hello Mrs. Kollin as cheerfully as I could and then step quickly over her bucket and soap and go inside and do something unnecessary to help push the thought of her down on her knees at her age from my mind.

Even looking at her working at other less strenuous jobs always gave me an uncomfortable feeling — a mixture of shame for her and guilt for myself, I suppose. When I say looking at her, I don't mean just with a glance but in the way you do on one of those occasions when you look at people you've known for a long time and really see them. I would see her line-marked face with its skin darkened from years of close contact with dust and dirt, her calm eyes with filmy cataracts edging over them, her infrequently washed hair, thin and dull, strained to a little bun at the back, the coarse grey threads falling round her face — and it would hurt me, and I would wish that I didn't see her.

Her hands used to disturb me too. They were bumpy at the joints so that people would ask her if she suffered from rheumatism to which she'd reply, no thank God, my fingers got like that from so much scrubbing on the washboard.

The round wrist bone above one of her hands stuck out in a knob ever since the time she fell down and broke her arm. She was walking home from our house one evening in early winter and she slipped on a little ice that had formed on the street and fell. Though it pained a bit that night, so she said, I don't believe she knew her arm was really broken until it was examined next day.

She went as an outpatient to the General Hospital to have it straightened and put in a splint. And I remember when we learned that she had spent all one day sitting on a hard bench at the hospital waiting to be attended to, how incensed our whole family was. We made critical remarks about all government institutions and about callous* young interns, and reminded ourselves of the dignity of the poor and the indignities they have to put up with. We said if Mrs. Kollin had been a wealthy woman she would have gotten attention quick enough and plenty of it.

All this we said again to Mrs. Kollin when she next came to the house, as she continued to do once a week because although she couldn't do much work for weeks and weeks she'd turn up as usual and sit in the kitchen and have a cup of tea and do some little job with her free hand. She hated to stay at home, she said, and do nothing....

As I was saying we commiserated* with Mrs. Kollin over the way she'd been neglected at the hospital. She agreed, mildly, as usual, with everything we said. Yes ma'am she said, or yes my dear. But she showed no resentment, not the

slightest. She wasn't really put out about it. And I began to
realize that she was never really put out about anything. That
was the remarkable thing about her. She'd always worked
hard, starting when she was very young, probably a mere child
and certainly when she should have been at school, for she
could neither read nor write. And she'd lost her husband early.
But nothing in life seemed too much for her. She was never
heard to grumble in all the forty years she worked for our
family. And we never heard her say an unkind word about
anyone. Occasionally she'd relay a bit of gossip, but she'd
always remain outside of it, never sitting in judgment. For
instance, one day she told us that a neighbour of hers had been
tut-tutting over the fact that another neighbour was already
going out with a man when her husband had only been in his
grave for six months. Her explanation, Mrs. Kollin's that is,
was I 'spose the poor soul's lonely.

She wasn't unhappy, Mrs. Kollin wasn't. She wasn't happy
either, in the sense of being aware of happiness. She just took
life as it was — not docilely accepting it, I don't mean, but just
partaking of it.

When I think of her in this way I feel very aware of how
difficult it is for people who are consciously thinking about
everything to be happy. Because a person like that is not
satisfied with taking life as it is, she must always be visualizing
a pattern in her living, so that she can stand off and look at it,
and see its general shape and reassure herself that it is
worthwhile. I suppose I am acting in that way in telling about
Mrs. Kollin and my association with her, working it all out to a
pattern as I see it.

But Mrs. Kollin wouldn't see it like that. It would never
occur to her to look for a pattern. She would simply get on with
her work.

I remember once my mother saying to her, "wouldn't you
like to take a few holidays, Mrs. Kollin?" Mrs. Kollin said,
"My dear, what would I be doing that for?" "To get a rest from
all your work," said my mother. "If I wasn't working," said
Mrs. Kollin, "I wouldn't be breathing...."

I often think of her...often.

Grace Butt

Grace Butt was born in Brigus. Her career as a teacher and a librarian have made her well-known in Newfoundland literary circles. As a playwright, she wrote the first full length Newfoundland play, **The Road Through Melton.** *Her plays have been produced in Dublin and on stage and radio in Canada. Her most recent dramatic work is* **Faces of Women.**

Understanding What You Have Read

1. Mrs. Kollin said, "If I wasn't working, I wouldn't be breathing." What do you think she meant exactly when she made this statement?

2. Did Mrs. Kollin think of housecleaning as work? When is work not "work"?

Things To Do

1. Think of people you have met in your community or elsewhere who have impressed you with their attitude toward life and work. Write a short narrative essay about your impressions of one such person.

2. Read "Sculpin" by Tom Dawe in *Baffles of Wind and Tide* and think about Old Adam's attitude toward life. Compare him to Mrs. Kollin.

* * *

Getting Ready To Read

Every society has its deserted villages, or ghost towns. In Newfoundland there are many deserted islands, where once there was active and energetic life. Georgiana Cooper describes such an island for us, painting vivid details of daily life there in the first half of her poem. In the second half we find the contrasting description of the island now that the people have gone. Bear in mind that this poem was written long before the days of the centralization policy of the fifties and sixties.

The Deserted Island

HERE in the years that were
Men walked with fishing gear —
Men brown'd and bearded.
Sturdily grown, and fearless
As the great rocks which stand
The battling of tumultuous seas.
Calloused their hands, and cupped
From rowing long against contrary winds.

Far seeing, kindly eyes and voices
Soft as the patter of summer rain —
And how they toiled! All the long season,
Early and late with fishtraps, hook and line,
Filling their stages full
With fish for Autumn selling.

Up the steep paths,
And by the dewy bracken* —
Past the blue flags,
And beds of cotton grass,
At eventide they come
To cheery homes made bright for their returning.

The busy wives — how sweet
They made those homes —
The gleaming lustre on the dresser hanging —
Soft to the tread the brightly coloured rugs
Spread o'er the well-scrubbed floors.
And restful beds of softest feathers
Plucked from the breasts of seabirds caught
for food.

And gardens, too, they made
Where flowers gave them joy —
Tall monkshood, bluebells,
Southern wood and roses,
And herbs, they grew —
And food to store away for winter eating.

Laughter and song
And stories strange and tragic
Were heard at many firesides
When neighbours gathered in;
And many moons smiled down
On many boys and girls,
Who softly walked with arms   vined
And faces radiant.

Now on those islands
There is only quiet,
No sound of human voice,
Save when a boat chugs out from land

To reap the grass which still
Grows lush along the hollows;
Or groups which come to picnic,
While the summer sunshine lingers.
There are no dwellings,
And by the water's edge, no wharves or stages.

No nets spread out for mending,
No hogsheads*, puncheons*, tubs or barrels,
No boats, no chains, or anchors —
All away —
Only the patient, ageless,
Rock-bound shores
To which all waves come in
Like children, shouting, whispering, sobbing;
Only this remains.

Through tangled scrub,
Bracken and wild berries,
Past the blue flag and cotton grass, I go,
And there, close by the crest,
With tall monkshood standing by
And sunshine flooding,
I read their names,
Cut deep in marble, slab on slab.

Georgiana Cooper

*Georgianna Cooper was born in 1885 in Inglewood Forest,
North West Arm, Trinity Bay. Her poem, "Lament for
Inglewood," deals with the resettlement undergone by the
people of this community. Her poems are found in* **The
Deserted Island.**

Understanding What You Have Read

1. Look for specific details which help us picture the island when it was alive.

2. Why do people still come to the island from time to time? Is there a deeper reason than the obvious?

3. The author suggests that some people remain on the island. Who are they? What is the significance of the phrase "cut deep in marble"?

Something To Do

1. The description of the island is a pleasant one. Look for a description of the harsher side of island living in "Moving Day" or "For Every Man An Island" in *Doryloads* or *Baffles of Wind and Tide*.

* * *

Peter Ball

The questions contained in the following poem make its pace (the rate at which the poem moves) quite deliberate. We are unable to read it quickly. The punctuation forces us to slow down as we read. Note that pace is a reflection of the title.

Old Soldiers

When I see soldiers passing
who were young
once
in a war
I am filled with open sadness
for their young days
gone before.
In each lined and wrinkled feature
hides a youth that once
they knew
when the sagging lips were firm
and the aiming eye
was true.
Steady fingers sent
lead bullets
smacking into flesh and bone
slashing off the days of some lad
longing in his fear
for home.
Are they not the real victors
those who cannot ever age
And are not the victors vanquished
as they march in their parades?
With their eye patches
and crutches
and their artificial limbs
are the living
not the losers
when the noise of battle dims?
I think war has only winners
in the ranks of those who died
and the ageing soldiers marching
are a kind of broken pride.

Paul O'Neill

"Paul O'Neill is among the best writers Newfoundland ever produced. He certainly has a way with words that is extraordinary." So wrote James R. Thoms in the **Daily News** *in 1976. By that time Paul O'Neill had written* **Spindrift and Morning Light** *(1969),* **The City In Your Pocket** *(1975),* **The Oldest City** *(1975),* **Legends of a Lost Tribe** *(1976), and* **A Seaport Legacy** *(1976). In addition he has published numerous writings in such books as* **East of Canada, Over the Horizon,** *and* **Rowboats and Rollerskates.** *During his career he has attended the National Academy of Theatre Arts in New York and acted with theatre groups around the world. He is presently the Executive Producer of Arts and General Programs with CBC television in St. John's. He was born in Bay de Verde in 1928.*

Understanding What You Have Read

1. Why do you think the poet would like you to read this poem slowly?

2. Do you agree with the poet's last thought in this poem? Why or why not?

Things To Do

1. Make a list of the appeals to the senses used in this poem and show how each is appropriate to the subject.

2. Read "Dulce et Decorum Est" by Wilfred Owen.

* * *

Ben Hansen

PEOPLE TOWARDS PEOPLE

PART I

No Comfort To Any Of Us

Prejudice exists wherever people live. We are not without it in this province. This unit explores and helps us understand various forms of prejudice. The word means to judge previous to having sufficient knowledge. The most obvious example of this is war, where one man seeks to kill another without even knowing him. Paul O'Neill explores that idea. Then there is the lack of understanding by one group of workers of the work and skills of those in a totally different occupation, as in the poem by Mary Sharpe. Even in a small community, or perhaps more often there, an individual who is different from others either physically or intellectually, is often misunderstood and shunned, as Noah is in Tom Dawe's poem. Ted Russell explores the attitudes and misunderstandings caused by geography, as he presents the views of the resident in relation to the tourist. Of course, religious discrimination has been with us for a long time, but we can be thankful that it is fast disappearing. But in the days of W.W. Wilson it was very much a fact, and we get some glimpse of the bitterness it created.

This poem is only one sentence. Like "Old Soldiers," it deals with those who have been called to fight in war. As we read this poem, however, we are struck by the contrast in pace between "Men Meeting" and "Old Soldiers." Try to figure out why this poem moves to its ending at a much faster rate than the previous one.

Men Meeting

He took in his traps
and went away
to where a war was
and
on a day he would have been
hauling cod in the bight
he took a gun
and shot down
another lad
in an enemy town where
they might have been laughing
and drinking beer
except that there was a war
that year.

Understanding What You Have Read

1. How does the author show the contrast between the scene at home and the scene at war?

2. Why do you think "Men Meeting" is written in just one sentence?

Things To Do

1. Interview a war veteran — maybe your grandfather or great-uncle. After your conversation write your own impressions either in poetry or prose form.

2. Read "The Man He Killed" by Thomas Hardy.

* * *

When people are taken out of their usual surroundings
and familiar situations they often become uncomfortable
and unsure of themselves. An observer may conclude that
such people are stupid and bumbling. In this poem a
fisherman is placed in the foreign environment of a
modern cafeteria, and is judged by the usual patrons of
the place. You should look beyond the obvious to try to
see what they do not see.

Old Man Ordering Tea

I remember
An old fisherman
Who looked ashamed,
Because he didn't know
The order of his tea.

I was furious,
That a cafeteria
Could do that
To a man
Whose brow was
Work sweat,
And whose blood was sea.

And the silly secretaries
In their metropolitan* minis*
Agreed
That he was indeed
A stupid man,
For slowing down
Their dinner line.

Mary Sharpe

Mary Sharpe is the director of psychiatric social work at the Waterford Hospital in St. John's, and has worked in several Newfoundland communities. She was born in Cormack, on Newfoundland's west coast, in 1948.

Understanding What You Have Read

1. This poem could easily end at the end of stanza two. What effect does the addition of the last stanza have?

2. Is the writer's use of the word "silly" in the last stanza an example of the kind of superficial judgments the poem is about?

Things To Do

1. Discuss how the secretaries might fare if they were placed in the fisherman's environment.

2. Can you think of other situations where such superficial judgments are made?

* * *

Getting Ready To Read

The speaker in "Noah" tells of a little boy, a "sissy", who grew up in the same community as the speaker did. Note the sad and quiet tone of the speaker's voice as he tries to explain why Noah could never be regarded as "one of us". Try to understand the uncomfortable effect Noah had on the speaker and his friends. But, most importantly, try to appreciate the poet's attempt to understand why people (like Noah) have such strange effects on us, or how they are like a "raven flying across a rainbow".

Noah

We could never regard him as one of us,
that little boy who made boats all summer
even though the puddle had dried up
and our town was miles from the sea.
He seemed to like the rain
when it did come,
that sissy who would sit inside
below his mother's breasts
reading story-books all day
and asking questions about the hills
above our town.
Once he came out near the end of a shower
and got all excited about some raven
flying across a rainbow.
He never killed frogs with us
when we sharpened summer spears
from the leafy twigs,
and he never owned a fishing pole.
Sometimes our parents made us
invite him to our birthday parties
and his parents forced him to come.
When he did arrive

he spent most of his time
staring through the window.
He was no comfort to any of us,
I can tell you that

Tom Dawe

Understanding What You Have Read

1. What unusual actions of Noah cause the speaker to say "We could never regard him as one of us"?

2. Why did Noah at the birthday party spend "most of his time/staring through the window"? Do you think Noah was sad because he wasn't one of the gang? Explain.

3. a) Noah "got all excited about some raven/flying across a rainbow". The speaker thought that was awfully odd of Noah. Do you? What would you have noticed more, the rainbow or the raven? Noah noticed both together. What does that suggest about the kind of person he was?

   b) In a poem words often have more meaning to them than just the obvious. So when reading a poem we have to think hard about not only what the words mean but also about what they suggest. Think about a "raven/flying across a rainbow". What do the words "rainbow" and "raven" suggest? If someone told you a raven flew across his/her rainbow, what could that person mean by such a phrase?

Things To Do

1. When a poet describes a scene or sight so vividly that we can see it in our imagination, we call the scene or sight a visual image. Write three visual images of your own.

2. "Noah" was taken from Tom Dawe's *Hemlock Cove and After.* Perhaps you would like to read this book.

* * *

Getting Ready To Read

Most accounts of tourists visiting a place are presented from the visitor's point of view. In the narrative essay which follows Ted Russell looks at the experience in a different way. He is more concerned with giving us the views of the local people. The usual point of view is reversed. This is an interesting literary move which helps the reader see the other side of the coin.

"Tourists" is an essay. The speaker is Uncle Mose, a principal character in Russell's 'Pigeon Inlet,' an imaginary Newfoundland community.

Tourists

Well, 'twill soon be the time when the round trippers or tourists, as the newspaper calls 'em, will be around again. Every time the coastal steamer anchors in Pigeon Inlet they'll be comin' ashore to stretch their legs, and to have a look at the place and see what kind of a crowd we are. And most of 'em will have their cameras and they'll take snapshots to show their friends back home in the Mainland part of Canada or the United States. Mind you, we're glad to see 'em, and I wouldn't say a word to hurt one of their feelings for anything. We do our best to answer their questions and to make them as welcome as we can. In fact, I hear tell as how they give us a good name afterwards for being hospitable. Yes, that's all very good as far as it goes. But today I'm goin' to make a remark or two about these round-trippers that I hope won't hurt any feelings, even if any of 'em happens to be listening. It's about these snapshots they take of Pigeon Inlet to show to their friends after they get back home.

There's a hummock on the Sou-Western side of Pigeon Inlet just behind Grampa Walcott's stage, and this hummock is a favorite spot for these people with their cameras. In the last five summers I've seen a hundred or more of 'em climb that hummock to take their snapshots. It seems that when they're on top of it the sun is always somewhere behind them and the whole waterfront is stretched out in a nice curved line right ahead of them so that they can get all the stages and the flakes in on the one snap.

Mind you, they can't get the church or the school or the Lodge or Aunt Sophy's fine boardin' house or any of the other nice-lookin' houses in the place, but they can get the stages and the flakes, and that seems to be the thing that interests 'em most, and the thing they're most anxious to show their friends back in Nova Scotia or Toronto or New York, or wherever they come from. Well, that's alright, only for one thing and that's the thing I want to mention.

You take the case of what happened here one day last August. I helped this lady — from New York she said she was — I helped her climb this hummock and she took her snapshots and was very pleased about it and thanked me very much for helping her. Then we got to talkin' about one thing and another. Then I asked her if she wasn't goin' to take any more snaps, of the school, or the church, or the Lodge or the children. She said no, because she said these things were much the same in Pigeon Inlet as they were anywhere else. But the stages and flakes, they was different, that's what Mainland people would be interested in. The things that were different — quaint and picturesque, she called them.

"Besides," she said, "we like to see where codfish come from. We eat codfish sometimes," she said.

Well, by this time I figgered I ought to say something.

"Ma'am," said I, "you've got nothin' against us people, have you?"

"Why, no," said she. "I like you people very much."

"And," said I, "you wouldn't like to do anything to hurt us, would you?"

"No," said she, "of course not. Why," said she, "will these photographs hurt you? Because," said she, "if I thought they could — "

"No, Ma'am," said I, "These snapshots won't hurt us. It's true these flakes and stages don't look very pretty in snaps and newspaper pictures. They're what you just said, 'quaint and picturesque.' But there it is, we've got 'em and we're not ashamed of 'em. The trouble is ma'am," said I, "they only tell half the story. They only show half the picture, and if you're going to show these pictures to people on the Mainland, you ought to tell 'em the rest of the story."

I could see she was interested, so I went on. "Tell 'em two things," said I. "In the first place, tell 'em that, apart from these quaint and picturesque things, the rest of Pigeon Inlet is much about the same as any small place anywhere on the Mainland. The children are just as pretty and well behaved, the houses just as clean and tidy and we grown-up folks — well, a bit ornery-lookin', but much about the same as people everywhere else."

"I'll certainly tell them that," said she. "What else?"

"Tell 'em this," said I. "Tell 'em that these flakes and stages got nothin' to do with any codfish they ever ate or are ever likely to eat."

"But," said she, "you use the flakes for dryin' fish, don't you?"

"Yes, ma'am," said I. "We use 'em for curin' fish for poor people — people in Europe and the West Indies. If we used anything more expensive, we might make the fish so dear that they wouldn't be able to afford to buy it. As it is, they can buy it but they don't pay much for it. That's why we're not very rich ourselves. But it's the best we can do for ourselves and for them."

"But," said she, "where does the fish come from we get?"

"Ah, ma'am," said I. "That's a different story. Next time," said I, "you're in places like St. John's or Burin or Bonavista or Harbour Grace — places like that, you just ask someone to take you to the fish plant and you'll see where your fish comes from. You'll see fine buildings, best kind of machinery, people workin' in spotless white uniforms. Take some snapshots of them, and tell your friends that that's where their fish comes from. I only wish," said I, "that by showin' them pictures of our fish plants you could persuade your friends to eat a lot more of our fish."

"Why?" said she

"Because then," said I, "we'd have more and more fish plants and less and less fish flakes. 'Tis nice bein' quaint and picturesque," said I. "The trouble is, there's not much money in it."

That woman wrote me a nice letter afterwards and told me about the lovely snaps she had got of a big fish plant on the

Southside of St. John's. She said 'twas as good as anything she'd ever seen in the States, and that she'd never have known anything about it if I hadn't put her on to it. She said the only thing she was sorry for was that she didn't have a snapshot of me to show her friends as a typical Newfoundland fisherman.

Well, what do you think of that?

Ted Russell

In the 1950s Edward Russell was known to many Newfoundlanders as Uncle Mose. Every week Uncle Mose was heard on CBC Radio's Fisheries Broadcast telling stories about characters and events in the imaginary outport of Pigeon Inlet. In these stories Russell tried to show the values possessed by ordinary Newfoundlanders whom he had come to know and respect through thirty years of working among them as a teacher and magistrate. During his career he worked in Millertown, Pass Island, Harbour Breton, Channel, Fogo and St. John's. He spent two years in the first cabinet formed by Premier Smallwood in 1949, but resigned on a point of principle. In addition to his Fisheries broadcast scripts, some of which have been published as **The Chronicles of Uncle Mose** *and* **Tales From Pigeon Inlet,** *Ted Russell wrote two plays:* **The Holdin' Ground** *and* **The Hangashore.** *Mr. Russell was born in 1904 and died in 1977.*

Understanding What You Have Read

1. Why did Uncle Mose think the tourist should take pictures of other things?

2. What effects do tourists have on an area like Pigeon Inlet?

Things To Do

1. Sketch the scene described in the second paragraph.

2. Give a good reason why the tourist wanted a picture of the flakes and stages rather than of the church or the lodge.

* * *

Getting Ready To Read

"Bonavista Circuit" is a story of prejudice and religious discrimination. It is an account of an attempt by a group of Episcopalians (Anglicans) to prevent the establishment of a Methodist (Wesleyan or United) Church in Bonavista. This article is an excerpt from W.W. Wilson's *Newfoundland and its Missionaries*, a history of the early Methodist Church in Newfoundland.

Prejudice is an irrational and unreasonable opinion leading to an unfair judgment. If you allow your prejudice to motivate your actions, you are being unjust. As you read "Bonavista Circuit" consider how religious prejudice led to a strong religious discrimination which became widespread in Newfoundland for many years. Traces of this may exist in some communities even today.

Bonavista Circuit

Bonavista is last on the list of stations. The distance of this place from St. John's is about one hundred miles. In consequence of the distance of Bonavista from Conception Bay, and the paucity* of missionaries, it was impossible to visit it, except occasionally. Our little church there, however, had been kept together by the faithful labors of two local brethren, Messrs. Saint and Cole, who in turn preached every Sabbath, and met the classes; but the appointment of a regular missionary to the Harbor was hailed by our people with great delight.

The population of Bonavista was estimated at about fifteen hundred souls, of whom three-fourths were Protestants; and the Episcopalians and Wesleyans were the only religious bodies among the Protestants.

The Episcopalians at that time never had a minister stationed among them; but they had a layman, who had formerly been a fisherman, authorized to read prayers on the Sabbath. He also baptized the children, and married the people.

As all the Protestants had been Churchmen, the introduction of Methodism was first looked upon with contempt; and then it was opposed, and afterward persecuted as far as the parties had the means. Opposition began most undisguisedly to show itself when a Wesleyan church was about to be erected, and a Wesleyan missionary stationed in the place. Our people, intent upon their object, braved all opposition, and put up their church, when the first open act of persecution occurred. It was in reference to the flag-staff placed in front of the building. The reader must be informed that, as there were no bells in the out-harbors, the signal for divine service was to haul up a flag in the front of the church, one hour before service began; drop it half-mast at the end of thirty minutes, and haul it down as the minister entered. As the Wesleyan church was nearly opposite to the Episcopal church, the officials of the latter intimated that it would be considered a gross insult, if the Methodists should dare to hoist a flag in the presence of their Episcopalian brethren; and that such an audacious* act should not be permitted. No notice was taken of this kind of talk, and when the church was fit for occupancy, our people proceeded to erect a flag-staff. The worthy magistrate, who was a zealous son of the Church, thought this was too bad, and he must put forth all his power and authority to prevent such an outrage. Was it not as much his business to stop the progress of Methodism as to keep the king's peace? Believing this to be his duty, he came over to the mission ground, and with much emphasis demanded:

What are you Methodists doing there?

Ans.   We are putting up a flag-staff.

Mag.   What do you want of a flag-staff there?

Ans.   To hoist a flag as a signal for divine service.

Mag.   What, directly opposite the church?

Ans.   We are not aware that we are doing any wrong.

Mag.   I tell you it shall not be, and I forbid it.

Ans.   We think you have no right to interfere with us, and we shall not regard your prohibition.

Mag.   Well, I will allow you to hoist your flag on any day but Sunday.

Ans.   That is the day on which we intend to hoist our flag.

Mag.   If you dare to hoist your flag on next Sunday, I will certainly cut it down.

The Sabbath came, and, regardless of his worship, the flag was raised at the appointed hour. As soon as our justice heard that the Methodist flag was up, he came in great wrath to punish such manifest contumacy.* He was accompanied by his son Jared, who was the constable, and who brought an axe to cut down the obnoxious flag-staff. Considerably excited, and a little out of breath, he said to the people who were now assembling for worship:

Did I not forbid your hoisting your flag on Sunday?

Ans.   You did; but we have not regarded your order, in this case, as we thought you had no right to interfere with us.

Mag.   I will let you Methodists know that I have power, and I will cut down the pole.

Calling to his son, he said, "Jared, cut down that flag-staff." The axe was raised, but ere the blow impinged the wood, Mr. Saint said, "Sir, take care what you do, for I have taken advice, and find we have done nothing wrong. If you will 'dare' to cut down the pole, I will give five pounds." At the sound of the word "advice", his worship was startled, and instantly called to his son to "stop"; and then addressing the people who were now assembled in considerable numbers, he said, "I will not cut down your flag to-day; but mind you never raise it again on Sunday."

His worship retired amidst the jeers of the people, and himself afterward taking "advice", he ascertained that he had gone too far, and therefore left the Methodists to hoist their flag whenever they thought proper.

The strange conduct and persecuting spirit of this Bonavista magistrate were afterwards satirized* in a piece of poetry, from which we extract the following:

Some few years ago, to our harbor there came
Some preachers from England; they're Methodists
                              by name;
They opposed our whole conduct, and said, 'Ye are
                              wrong;
Repent, or ye'll perish,' was the theme of their song.
A chapel and flag-staff they soon did erect,
Though 'gainst Bonavist law it was levelled direct;
'I'll cut down your flag-staff,' said one then in
                              power,
'If you raise up your flag at the specified hour.'

This petty persecution did Methodism no harm, and the labors of Brother James Hickson were greatly blessed. Our church was quickened and consolidated, and it has continued to prosper ever since.

W.W. Wilson

Reverend William Wilson wrote a history of Methodism in Newfoundland entitled **Newfoundland and its Missionaries.** *He was a nineteenth century clergyman who served in Newfoundland.*

Understanding What You Have Read

1. Why did the local magistrate feel it was his job to prevent the construction and use of a flag-staff by the Methodists?

2. What did the flag-staff represent to the Episcopalians? What did it come to represent for the Methodists?

Things To Do

1. Discuss some of the effects of religious prejudice in any community.

2. Are you aware of other types of prejudice? List some.

* * *

PEOPLE TOWARDS PEOPLE

PART II
Look After Number One

Even the best of people have a certain selfishness in them. It's part of human nature. But sometimes it happens that selfishness or a self-centered attitude will have a great effect on ourselves or others. Percy Janes lets see how selfishness in a husband destroys the woman he once loved, and, we suspect, has embittered the man as well. Enos Watts shows us how self-indulgence and a habit of justifying a dangerous practice lead to self-destruction. And Ted Russell lightens the mood a little, showing how taking time and reflecting on the consequences to himself helps a man continue living as he wishes.

Justin Hall

Getting Ready To Read

A good writer will often prepare his readers for any turn of events in a story. The hints or clues which he gives throughout the plot are called foreshadowing. Many clues about Joe Saunder's values and character are given before you ever meet him. Watch for them.

Curtains

Sometimes May Saunders felt she was not long for this world. She could tell by the sudden breath-stopping pain that took her now and then like pincers in the left side of her chest; and also by a strange feeling of remoteness that often came over her, as if the life around her and even in her own home were no more than a film being unrolled for her benefit but at a great distance.

The attack had come only recently: it was the first real illness she had ever had and was all the harder to bear in that she was still, by her own count, on the right side of middle age and always thought of herself as a healthy, active woman — one who would easily be able to bear whatever burdens life might choose to put upon her. These burdens were not light, being mainly six children, the eldest a daughter named Ellen aged sixteen and no longer in school, and the youngest not much more than a baby just out of arms. Yet after she had been hit with this illness May found that her strength seemed to pass away like spring water, so that it was not long before, from being house-bound, she was bed-ridden by her weakness, and fretting quite as much as any busy wife and mother would in these circumstances. She simply could not accept the idea of being laid up like this in the prime of her strength, doing nothing; but those agonizing warnings were coming so insistently that the doctor had ordered absolute rest for at least three months.

Apart from the five youngest children, who had been bundled in with neighbors during this critical time, May had only two other great preoccupations or longings as she lay passing the weary hours in her bed: she had never really understood her husband Joe; and in all the years of her married life she had never had any new curtains for her bedroom. Now she felt it almost as a premature doom, having to lie all alone from dawn to dawn (her husband was sleeping in the children's room since she had been taken so bad) staring at those dismal old curtains that in colour had once been magenta but over the years had slowly faded to a bilious* shade of pink that was enough to poison you just to look at it. They had been a wedding present from Joe's mother.

As for her husband, Joe Saunders was a poor man, and that she had never held against him, but he was also as mean as a weasel. He was always complaining about any little extra item she put on the budget and fretting over how much they had, or did not have, in the bank. Once he had returned a small bathroom mat she had bought on sale at Woolworth's for 79¢ and tried to get his money back. He came home furious after being told there was no refund on sale goods. It was only a short time later that he had announced his intention of taking over the household money and spending it himself and this was the first time in her marriage that she had really had to put her foot down.

In a rather vague fashion May hoped that now she was ill and helpless, he might show another side of his nature and in their new intimacy she would really begin to understand him, get to the bottom of his character and know him as all her women friends boasted they knew their men inside out, to the point of being able to tell what they intended to do or how they would take a certain thing in married life, long before the men knew it themselves. But here the first move would have to come from Joe: it was up to him to show that he was something more than the most casual of fathers and a not too bountiful provider.

To satisfy her other longing — that of redecorating her bedroom at least to the point of brightening up the window — May was able to do something herself, or at least with Ellen's help; and one dark mawsy* morning she made up her mind to act, no matter how much it might cost or what kind of a fuss Joe would make when he found out about it.

The very last time May had been downtown she had noticed some gorgeous green material at Woolworth's, for a price that seemed to her reasonable as things went these shockingly expensive days. Now she called Ellen and, after describing the material carefully and giving the exact price as it had appeared on the cloth, told her to go down and get two lengths if they were still there, charging it to the Saunders account. Ellen, a girl whom everybody declared to be as sensible as an old grandmother, would not even leave the house without having arranged for someone to stay with her mother, but this was soon settled with the neighbor who already had the other children; and so in less than an hour Ellen had made the return trip from Livingstone Street to Water Street, and rushed eagerly into her mother's bedroom with the large parcel in her arms.

The two of them began to enjoy this little plot they had hatched and were carrying out so successfully. First, May had Ellen take one length of the material and hold it up against the wall near the window. Yes, it seemed to be all right. Even after the time that had passed since she had been at Woolworth's and all that had happened since then, May's memory and judgment and taste had not failed her. That was a good sign. The deeply rich forest-green colour of the new material was exactly right against her cream walls and the off-white ceiling. Now she ordered her daughter to rip down those old curtains and throw them in the garbage. Then, as eager as a child in mischief, she had Ellen wheel the sewing machine into her bedroom and hitched herself up in bed to supervise her while she carefully hemmed the curtains at the bottom to proper length and at the top so that the old-fashioned rods would easily pass through and let them hang gracefully.

The moment of trial, when Ellen had the curtains up and their full effect could be seen, was a golden moment for May — so much so that suddenly she felt tears coming into her eyes, and inwardly reproved herself for this foolishness. Yet she could not help it: the least little emotion made her cry these days. She supposed it would go away as soon as her strength came back and she was herself again. And the curtains really were perfect! They were more like drapes, in fact, with that wealth of texture and their generous length. Her bedroom was transformed, and the satisfaction May took in this triumph over all the drab, toiling years of her married life, as well as some humiliations in that time, was inexpressible. She kissed Ellen in gratitude and sent her out to the kitchen to fetch a glass of water so that she could take one of her heart pills on schedule.

And now she had to pay for all this excitement and exertion. Hardly had Ellen left the room when May was seized by another attack of that searing pain. Her heart felt like an animal leaping up into her throat, pushing to get out of captivity, and all at once her bed became a boat that swirled back and forth, up and down in a crazy switchback way that made her feel as sick as if she really had been out on a stormy ocean. It was all gravity pull and no anchor. May was now sweating with the pain, and she fell back on her disarranged pillows as weak as wet paper.

She thought she was going to pass out, or worse; but she was aware of Ellen when the girl came back into the room and could hear a gasp of surprise and fright when their eyes met in this new situation. She also tried to co-operate as Ellen started to give her the pill. It was no use. May gagged and coughed out the nasty cylindrical capsule as if it had been poison. Then she felt Ellen touching and trying to comfort her before rushing out to the telephone.

Ellen was almost screaming in her anxiety to get help, so May could easily hear her begging to speak to the doctor himself and, when he was apparently not available, insisting that in this case the family doctor must make a house call because it was a real emergency. Desperate, Ellen seemed to get her way, for she came back to her mother and spoke to her reassuringly about help coming real soon.

When the doctor did arrive he took one look at the patient, went through one or two of his routines such as listening to her heart, checking her pupils, and feeling her hands and feet for circulation and warmth. At this point May caught him beckoning to Ellen to come outside the room, obviously so that they might speak in private. Her senses made more acute by illness, and her fear hanging on every word, May heard the doctor say that perhaps Ellen should call her father, and maybe also their minister . . . ah . . . just in case. Ellen got on the phone again.

Not long afterwards May heard a clatter at the back of the house and knew by the typical sounds that her husband had preceded the minister. He had come quickly, then, in spite of his habit of stopping off with the boys on his way home from the CN dockyard where he worked. She hardly knew how she felt about his arriving first, and did not have long to ponder it, because after a few hurried words with the doctor Joe Saunders could be heard clumping towards the bedroom and entering awkwardly, his step made slow perhaps and his manner hesitant by the gravity of the situation.

As he came closer to the bed his wife made an effort and turned her head to face him. She was met first of all by the sour, yeasty reek of regurgitated* beer that was Joe's characteristic smell and hung about him more or less permanently like a body odour. It was the most distasteful thing about her husband that she had had to conquer and accept many years before — if their marriage were to continue. Perhaps he might do or say something now to make up for this and many other shortcomings.

But before Joe got right up to the bed May dimly saw him stop with a jerk, his eyes veer off and fix as if he had suddenly been paralyzed. She followed his gaze, and realized that it was resting on the strange drapes at the window. He began to breathe more heavily.

Now May was fully aware of him and could hear him distinctly as he strode up to the bedside, bent over her and bawled out in a raucous, protesting tone, at the same time making a thrusting gesture of non-responsibility with his left arm: "Look here, May! Look here. If you dies, I'm not payin' for them new curtains!"

Percy Janes

Percy Janes, who was born in 1922, won wide recognition in 1970 with the publication of **House of Hate,** *a novel which explores the origins and the destructive power of hate within a family. Mr. Janes was educated in Corner Brook, St. John's and Toronto, and served for four years with the Canadian Navy during World War II. He lived in England for several* *years before returning to Newfoundland in 1973. In addition to* **House of Hate** *he has published* **So Young and Beautiful** *(1958) and numerous poems and short stories.*

Understanding What You Have Read

1. a) Is the ending of this story a surprise to the reader?
   b) Is the ending believable? Why, or why not?

2. Early in the story the reader begins to identify with May and her situation. By what means does the author accomplish this?

Things To Do

1. Discuss the suitability of the title.

2. Think of other characters you have read about who have similiar traits. Can they help themselves in any way? The wife or husband of such an individual can be either a help or a hinderance. Explain.

* * *

Ben Hansen

Getting Ready To Read

Have you ever intently observed a person, especially an old-timer "sucking" on an unfiltered cigarette such as a Players or a MacDonald's? Did that person, like the character in "MacDonald's Plain", have a distinctive way of holding the cigarette, between say the "thumb and the index"? Did he draw in on the cigarette "with concentrated concavity of the face", as though the smoke would give him "dear-life"?

The poet in "MacDonald's Plain" gives a clear picture of a smoker in two contrasting situations. He also gives us a glimpse of how a person can justify behaviour which is known to be harmful or dangerous.

"MacDonald's Plain" is an example of free verse poetry. Free verse is poetry with no regular rhyme or beat. However, to create a likeness to beat, the poet carefully chooses words and line lengths. As well the poet creates strong images (pictures) from careful word choice. As you read the poem be aware of words and images used to create a special feeling and present a special message.

MacDonald's Plain

He had a certain way
of holding the Export roll-your-own
between stained thumb and index
gripping it for dear-life
and with concentrated concavity*
of the face
(not thinking about
the Surgeon General's Report)
he would draw the fire toward him
faster than an ordinary man

It was on such an occasion
that he took most pride

in the longevity* of his ancestry
all the time reminding
young health-cultist* types
that Sister So-and-So
had never touched it
but she had been put under ground
for something-or-other
of the lungs
ten years ago

Last night
I saw
under the tent
the unconcentrated concavity
of his face
holding on for dear-life
drawing the oxygen into him
faster than an ordinary man

There was no perceptible*
stirring
of the stained thumb and index
on the white linen

Enos Watts

Enos Watts is presently living with his wife and children in Stephenville, Newfoundland, where he is the vice-principal of W.E. Cormack Academy. Born in 1939 at Long Pond, Manuels, he has lived in many Newfoundland communities. His poems "Looking Back" and "Precision" reflect his sense of heritage, while all of his poetry reveals a deep understanding of and feeling for the human condition. Mr. Watts has written one book of poems entitled **After the Locusts,** *and his poetry has been published in Canadian and American magazines.*

Understanding What You Have Read

1. What are the *two* meanings contained in the line "draw the fire toward him faster than an ordinary man"?

2. Why do you think that on "such an occasion" the smoker "took most pride in the longevity of his ancestry"?

3. In the third sentence of the poem Watts has only a few words different from those used in the first sentence, yet the common words create a completely different image or picture. Explain how the situation of the smoker is different in sentence three.

4. What do the phrases "no perceptible stirring" and "the white linen" foreshadow (predict)?

Things To Do

1. Write a paragraph in which you give and explain several reasons why you think people smoke.

2. Read more of Enos Watt's poetry in *Baffles of Wind and Tide* and *After the Locusts.*

* * *

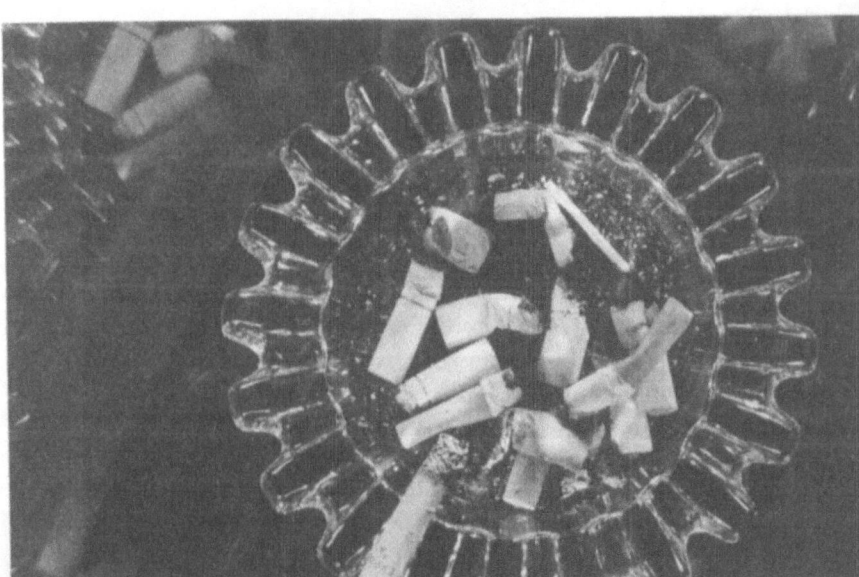

Getting Ready To Read

The following essay is just one of many by the late Ted
Russell, who created an imaginary outport called Pigeon
Inlet and peopled it with interesting characters who were
typical of the real people living in Newfoundland during
the forties and fifties. In stories such as "Letter to Aunt
Sophy" the author uses satire in a very mild and gentle
way. In using satire an author may create characters who
have vices or faults or prejudices that are present in many
real people. In revealing these vices the writer helps the
readers to see and understand people in a new and more
observant way. In this selection Russell uses Aunt Sophy
for satiric purposes. As you read think about the kind of
person Aunt Sophy represents and the effect she has in
trying to change a man's nature.

Letter To Aunt Sophy

Well, I almost took the plunge one night late last March. I was
sittin' by myself in the kitchen this night about nine o'clock,
with my boots off, a pair of woolen vamps* hauled on over my
socks, and with my feet up on the pan of the stove smokin' my
pipe, comfortable as anything but lonesome. My mind was on
Aunt Sophy.

I had a letter from Aunt Sophy that day. She's been writin'
me one every mail from Corner Brook this winter, but this
letter seemed kind of special. Not that there was anything a
man could put his finger on, but readin' kind of between the
lines as you might say, 'twas a different kind of letter from the
others. There was one place in it where she said not to tell her
father and mother (that's Grampa and Grandma Walcott), but
she said she missed me just as much as she missed them.
Perhaps even more, she said, but she had the "perhaps even
more" crossed out, though you could still read it right plain.
Well, there was several more things like that. So, bein' kind of
lonesome like I said, they affected me. After all, a man can't
help his nature.

So I had just answered her letter and my answer was a bit
special, too. Generally speakin', all my letters to Aunt Sophy
have been along the lines that everybody uses. I've said, "Dear

Aunt Sophy. Just a few lines to let you know that I am well and I hope you are the same. Thank God for it." Stuff like that. Good sensible stuff. A man can fill out two or three pages with that kind of stuff and not say anything he'd have to answer for later.

But this time, feelin' as I was, like I said, I wrote a different kind of an answer altogether. Naturally, I won't tell you what I wrote — that's private business. But it started "Dear Aunt Sophy. I miss you something awful and can hardly wait for the first steamer to come in the spring and bring you back to those who has such a regard for you." And it went right on from there for two full pages of an Exercise Book. Then I sealed it up all ready to post before the mail closed next mornin'.

Just then, who should come in but Skipper Joe Irwin. Skipper Joe has been comin' in two or three nights every week the winter for a smoke or a yarn or a game of cribbage or to listen to the hockey matches from St. John's. We've been interested in hockey ever since we listened to the Canadians beat the Russians, and Skipper Joe is catchin' on to cribbage so well, and gets so much luck that it's takin' me all my time to beat him.

"Is the hockey game on?" said Skipper Joe after he got settled away in front of the stove with his pipe goin', too.

"I dunno," said I. "Turn on the radio and see." So Skipper Joe reached over and turned it on. The game wasn't on, but the stuff that was on was enough to make a man lose his appetite. All about women, cryin' about how much they love somebody and how much somebody didn't love them. Foolishness like that.

"Mary's other husband's wife," said Skipper Joe.

"Turn it off, quick," said I. "Foolishness."

"Yes," said Skipper Joe, "that's been on now for four or five years. Looks like they'll never get it settled."

"I wonder who listens to the trash?" said I.

"Women," said Skipper Joe.

"Oh," said I.

Then Skipper Joe and myself played the best two out of three at cribbage, and for all his luck, I won the beater. Then

Skipper Joe was gettin' up to go home, but I persuaded him to set fast while I got a couple of glasses and rooted round till I found something to fill 'em up with. Skipper Joe slopped some of his over the table by accident but I told him 'twas no difference so long as the cards didn't get wet. I went off to freshen up his glass for him. When I come back out of the pantry, he had just finished moppin' up the stuff off the table and I noticed he couldn't help seein' the letter addressed to Aunt Sophy. He said nothin' at the time, but a few minutes later after we'd had a swig or two out of the glasses and pipes lighted again, he cleared his throat.

"Uncle Mose," he said.

"Yes, Skipper Joe?" said I.

Skipper Joe took another swig and a few more puffs before he answered me.

"Uncle Mose," he said, "you know I'm a man what minds his own business."

"That's right, Skipper Joe," said I, wonderin' what was comin'.

"And," said he, "I'm not a man what pokes his nose in where 'tis not wanted."

"Of course you're not," said I, and now I was more puzzled than ever to know what he was drivin' at.

Well, whatever it was he was drivin' at seemed to be botherin' him a lot. I noticed every time before he said anything else, he had to take another swig, like it was givin' him courage to go on. And, of course, every time he'd take a swig, I'd take one for good manners.

"Uncle Mose," he said, "you won't take offence at what I'm goin' to say?"

"No, Skipper Joe," said I.

"And, of course," he said, after we'd had another swig, "whatever is said won't go any further?"

"Of course it won't," said I.

"Uncle Mose," he said, "about you and Aunt Sophy. "

"Yes," said I.

"Is anything comin' of it?" said he.

" 'Tis quite possible," said I.

"A weddin' ?" said he.

"Possible," said I.

"In the fall of the year?" said he.

"Likely time," said I. Then, "Skipper Joe," said I. "What do you think of the idea?"

"Uncle Mose," said he, "like I said, I'm a man that minds me own business. Now," he said, "I must be off home. Goodnight, boy."

But I wouldn't let him go as easy as that. He had me worried by this time. I had answered his question and now he had to answer mine and tell me what he thought about the idea of me and Aunt Sophy makin' a match. What was wrong with it? I freshened our glasses again.

"Now, Skipper Joe," said I. "Man to man. Out with it. Why shouldn't I marry Aunt Sophy?"

"I didn't say you shouldn't marry her," said Skipper Joe.

"No," said I. "But you're thinkin' it. Now what's the reason?"

Skipper Joe had to take a longer swig than usual this time before he could answer.

"Uncle Mose," he said, "I got nothin' in the world to say against Aunt Sophy. She's a wonderful woman."

"That's good," said I. "Go on!"

"And, Uncle Mose," he said, "she'll make you a wonderful missus. Just the kind of a woman you need," said he, "to straighten you up a bit."

"To straighten me up," said I. "What do you mean, straighten me up? Ain't I straightened up enough now?"

"Enough to suit yourself," said Skipper Joe. "And enough to suit me. But perhaps not enough to suit Aunt Sophy. You see, Uncle Mose," said Skipper Joe, "I knew her husband, poor George Watkinson, before he died. She made a man out of him alright."

"Oh?" said I. "Wasn't he a man all the time?"

"Yes," said Skipper Joe, "he was. But she made a better one out of him. She changed him. You know — straightened him up. I watched it goin' on for years."

"What did she do to him?" said I.

"A lot of things," said Skipper Joe. "First of all, there was his moustache. A fine moustache he had, too. Much like yours."

"What in the world did she do with his moustache?" said I.

"Made him shave it off," said Skipper Joe.

"No!" said I.

"Yes," said Skipper Joe. "He rebelled for a while. Said he'd feel like a fool without it, and half-naked besides. But she made him shave it off, just the same."

"How did she make him?" said I.

"Soup," said Skipper Joe. "Aunt Sophy always made good soup and poor George used to brag about it. Well, one day Aunt Sophy laid down the law. Either he shaved off his moustache or — no more soup, so he broke down and shaved it off."

"Perhaps," said I, "she's changed her mind about moustaches since."

"No," said Skipper Joe. "I've heard her say many a time since that she'd couldn't bear a man with a moustache or she said if a man of hers had one, he wouldn't have it long. Poor George felt bad about losin' his. I used to pity him rainy nights when he'd come into my house to smoke his pipe before goin' to bed."

"Why would he come rainy nights?" said I.

"Well," said Skipper Joe, " 'twas like this. Aunt Sophy didn't like tobaccy smoke too well, but she'd put up with it, provided George was tidy about it. But if ever he wasted pipe ashes on the floor or around the stove, she'd lay down the law again — no smokin' in the house for two weeks. So he'd go outdoors for a smoke and rainy nights he'd come into my house for shelter and to ease his feet."

I looked at the pipe ashes on the pan of the stove. "Ease his feet?" said I.

"Yes," said Skipper Joe. "He used to like to wear vamps like you're wearin', but she said no. Vamps and soft slippers are catch-alls for dust and dirt. So he had to wear shiny-hard ones with elastic sides. Poor George. He used to be glad to sit down in my kitchen in his stockin'-feet and wiggle his toes to get the circulation back in 'em."

Skipper Joe took another swig, so big that I had to freshen up his glass again.

"Yes," said Skipper Joe, "Aunt Sophy is a remarkable woman. I'll bet," he said, "I know what she was doin' tonight."

"What?" said I.

"Listenin' to the radio," said Skipper Joe. "Listenin' to that program we turned off. That one about Mary's other husband's wife. She never misses it."

"How do you know?" said I.

"Because," said Skipper Joe, "any time she misses a chapter on account of a meetin', she always gets my missus next mornin' to tell her what happened. Poor George, her husband," said Skipper Joe, "it used to drive him half-cracked."

"But," said I, "that program wasn't on fifteen years ago."

"Yes, it was," said Skipper Joe, "only it had another name then. Instead of 'Mary's other husband's wife,' they used to call it 'John's other wife's husband.' But if there was any difference, 'twas all the same."

Skipper Joe was just goin' through the door when he turned round. "Mose," he said, "I'll wish you much joy of Aunt Sophy. Course," he said, "I'll miss our games of cribbage."

"Why?" said I.

"Aunt Sophy can't bear it," said Skipper Joe. "She says she's listened to her boarders playin' it and all this nonsense about fifteen-two and fifteen-four drives her wild. Good night, Uncle Mose," said he and was gone.

I sat there for a long time and pondered. I looked at the nice homely mess on the pan of the stove, the two dirty glasses on the table, and the stain where Skipper Joe had only partly mopped up what he'd wasted. I wiggled my toes in my old woolen vamps and glanced up at the radio on the shelf, where Mary's other husband and all the rest of 'em were locked in and couldn't get out unless I let 'em.

Then I picked up the letter I'd wrote Aunt Sophy, read it over again, shook my head a time or two and stuffed it between the bars in the front of my stove. Reaching for my pen, ink and exercise book, I stroked my moustache a time or two to make sure 'twas still there, and started another letter. It started like this:

"Dear Aunt Sophy: Just a few lines to let you know that I am well and I hope you are the same. Thank God for it."

Like I said, good sensible stuff with nothin' in it that a man would have to answer for.

Ted Russell

Understanding What You Have Read

1. a) What does the author mean by "I almost took the plunge" in the opening paragraph?
   b) What significance does "lonesome", first used in the opening paragraph, come to have as the story develops?

2. a) What vices of Aunt Sophy does Skipper Joe Irwin dwell on?
   b) What is ironic about Skipper Joe's statement "Aunt Sophy is a remarkable woman!"?

Things To Do

1. If you enjoyed "Letter to Aunt Sophy" you might like to read Ted Russell's *Tales From Pigeon Inlet* and *The Chronicles of Uncle Mose.*

2. Read the biographical note on Ted Russell which appears at the end of "Tourists" on page 103 .

* * *

Native Labradorian speaking out at public hearings
David Wegenast / DECK'S AWASH

NATIVE PEOPLES

In this short unit we look at three pieces related to the capture of Demasduit, the wife of the last Beothuck chief. This incident in Beothuck history is chosen because it resulted in the death of Nonosabasut, leaving them without a leader. From that point the doom of the people was sealed. The first two pieces are more or less historical accounts, but the piece by Stella Whelan is creative writing from the present time. Students will have to try to come to some kind of understanding of the circumstances which resulted in this great tragedy.

In Labrador Martin Martin represented his people, the Inuit, with pride and wisdom. We are permitted to listen to some of his thoughts about living together with others in this province, and the vital importance of understanding our own heritage.

Getting Ready To Read

The Beothucks are recognized as the principal inhabitants of the island of Newfoundland at the time of white settlement. It is probable that their numbers never increased beyond a few hundred, but they moved freely across the island. As more and more settlers claimed more and more of the island, the Beothucks were forced into smaller and smaller areas in which they had to find enough fish and animals to subsist on. This proved very difficult. Death by diseases, such as tuberculosis, brought by the European settlers, and by violence between the Beothucks and these settlers, greatly reduced the number of Beothucks. By the early eighteen hundreds the population of Beothucks consisted of less than one hundred people, surviving mainly in the Red Indian Lake to Notre Dame Bay area. And yet, after almost three hundred years of contact, no communication or cooperation existed between them and the settlers.

Concerned by this absence of communication and cooperation, and moved by a humane concern about the possible extinction of the Beothuck race, the Governor of Newfoundland, K.G. Keats, in 1813 proclaimed that the Beothucks were now under royal protection and he offered a reward of one hundred pounds (roughly several thousand of today's dollars) for anyone who could establish friendly contact with the Beothucks.

In response to this, and because a small group of Beothucks had stolen guns, sails and other items from his boat in Exploits, Notre Dame Bay, John Peyton Jr. of Twillingate, in March of 1819, led a group of fur trappers and fishermen up the Exploits River to Red Indian Lake to try to locate the Beothucks.

The following extract from a letter by John Peyton Jr. to the Governor of Newfoundland describes his journey, and how he captured a Beothuck woman named Demasduit, the wife of the Beothuck chief, Nonosabasut.

In reading this extract, you must keep in mind that it is a letter which, like a diary and an autobiography, presents only one side of a story, one point of view — a very subjective picture. As you read you must remember that John Peyton Jr. is describing events as he saw them and/or as he would like for other people to see them. You, like a judge, must try to separate facts from opinions, and make your judgment based on facts rather than on opinion. However, despite its subjective nature, John Peyton's letter will prove to be an interesting description of the Beothucks and the tension existing between them and the white settlers.

The Capture of Demasduit
(John Peyton's Narrative)

On the first of March, 1819, I left my house accompanied by my father and eight of my own men with a most anxious desire of being able to take some of the Indians and thus through them open a friendly communication with the rest. Everyone was ordered by me not upon any account to commence hostilities without my positive orders. On the second of March we came upon a few wigwams frequented by the Indians during the spring and autumn for the purpose of killing deer. On the third we saw a fireplace by the side of the brook where some Indians had slept a few days before. On the fourth, at ten o'clock, we came to a storehouse belonging to the Indians. On entering it I found five of my cat traps, set, as I supposed, to protect their venison from the cats. From the fireplace and tracks on the snow we were convinced the Indians had left the day before in the direction southwest. We therefore followed their footing with all possible speed and caution. At eleven o'clock we left the greatest part of our provisions in order to make more speed, as we were expecting to come up to them very soon. At one o'clock we came to a path where they entered the woods leading away about north northeast. At two o'clock we saw where they had slept the night before; we continued to travel till dark. On the fifth, we commenced walking as soon as it was day. At eight we came to a large brook which ran about southwest. We followed the course of the water which brought us into a very large pond but the wind, blowing a heavy drift, had destroyed all signs of the tracks; after travelling about one and a half miles I discovered the quite fresh footings of two or more Indians. We imagined they were gone into the woods for the purpose of partridge shooting, so I ordered the men to keep close together and keep a good lookout towards the woods. On proceeding a little further I saw a high point projecting on the pond, and on looking over it very carefully I discovered one Indian coming towards us, and three more going the contrary way at some considerable distance. I fell back and told our party what I had seen. Their curiosity being excited I could not restrain them from endeavouring to get sight of the Indians. I was not then certain there were no more in the same course I saw the one in. I could not tell at this time whether the Indian I saw was a male or female. I showed myself openly on the point. When the Indian discovered me she, for a moment, was motionless. She screamed out as soon as she appeared to make me out and ran off. I immediately pursued her, but did not gain on her until I had taken off my rackets and jacket. As I came up quickly to her she kept looking back at me over her shoulder. I then dropped my gun on the snow and held up my hands to show her I had no gun. She stopped, I did the same and endeavoured to convince her I would not hurt her. I then advanced and gave her my hand and she gave hers to me and to all my party as they came up. We then saw seven or eight Indians repeatedly run off and on the pond. Shortly after three Indians came running towards us. When they came within about two hundred or three hundred yards from us they made a halt. I advanced towards them with the woman, and on her calling to the Indians two of their party came down to us. A third halted again about one hundred yards distant. I ordered one of the men to examine one of the Indians that did come down to us, having observed something under his cassock, which proved to be a hatchet which the man took from him. The other two Indians then came and took hold of my arms endeavouring to force me away from the woman. I cleared myself as well as I could still having the woman in my hand. The Indian from whom the hatchet was taken attempted to lay hold of three different guns, but without effect. He, at last, succeeded in getting hold of my father's gun and tried to force it from him, and in the attempt to get his gun he and my father got off nearly fifty yards from me in the direction of the woods. The Indian grasped my father by the throat. My father drew a bayonet with the hope of intimidating the Indian. It had not the desired effect, for he only made a savage grin at it. I then called for one of the men to strike him which he did across the hands with his gun, but the Indian still held on to my father till he was struck on the head, when he let my father go. Then he either struck at or made a grasp at the man who struck him, which the man evaded by falling under the Indian's hand. The Indian then turned again on my father and made a grasp at his throat. My father freed himself and on his retreat, the Indian still forcing him, fired. The rest of the Indians fled immediately on the fall of the unfortunate one.

J.P. Howley

Adapted

J.P. Howley, a geologist, was born in 1847 and died in 1918. Mr. Howley was a graduate of St. Bon's in St. John's and studied under the well-known Newfoundland geologist, Alexander Murray. He is author of **Beothucks or Red Indians (The Aborigine People)** *and* **The Geology of Newfoundland.**

Understanding What You Have Read

1. What actions of the Beothucks reveal the frustration and dismay caused by the capture of Demasduit? Does this frustration and dismay reveal anything about the kind of people the Beothucks were?

2. Why was one Beothuck more determined than the others to secure the release of Demasduit? What was the consequence of his actions? Was this justified?

3. Why were the Beothucks so fearful of Peyton's men who were so few and so far into Beothuck territory? What was the result of their fear?

4. John Peyton captured Demasduit to help to establish communication and co-operation betwen the Beothucks and the European settlers. Was this a good way to establish communication and co-operation? Why or why not?

Things To Do

1. Write a full description of the appearance and actions of the white man from the point of view of a Beothuck.

2. Read Al Pittman's poem, "Shanawdithit" in *Baffles of Wind and Tide*.

* * *

Original portrait of March March, painted by Lady Hamilton in 1819 (Public Archives of Canada, Ottawa, C87698). Reprint from the **Newfoundland Quarterly,** *Spring 1980 (article by Christian Hardy and Ingeborg Marshall).*

Getting Ready To Read

"Demasduit" is an abridgement (a rewritten and
shortened version) of an article written by a Sir Hercules
Robinson, the commander of the British ship *HMS
Favourite* which was serving in Newfoundland waters
around the time of Demasduit's capture and her forced
visitation to St. John's. Sir Robinson probably never met
Demasduit (he calls her Mary March), so his article is
based on information obtained from Mr. Leigh in whose
residence Demasduit stayed before she was transported
by John Peyton Jr. to see the Governor at St. John's.

The following description of her capture and
captivity begins where the previous selection concluded.
This selection, like the previous one, is written from a
very subjective point of view. The description of the
character and personality of Demasduit conveys one
man's impression of what he believed to be a very brave
woman maintaining courage and dignity despite great
personal tragedy and grief.

Demasduit

The tribe being in the neighbourhood of this disastrous
meeting, it was necessary that the party should secure their
retreat. They had a sleigh drawn by dogs in which Mary
March, as she was afterwards named, immediately placed
herself. When she understood she was to accompany the party,
she directed them by signs to cover her over, holding her legs
out to have her moccasins laced. Both here and subsequently,
by the attention she appeared habitually to expect at the hands
of others, and by her unacquaintance with any laborious
employment, she indicated either a superiority of station, or
that she was accustomed to a treatment of female savages very
different from that of all other tribes.

She was tall and rather stout; her limbs were very small and
delicate, particularly her arms. Her hands and feet were very
small and beautifully formed, and of these she was very proud.
Her complexion, a light copper colour, became nearly as fair
as a European's after a course of washing and absence of
smoke; her hair was black and she delighted to comb and oil it;

her eyes, large and intelligent; her teeth, small, white and regular; her cheek bones, rather high; her voice, remarkably sweet, low and musical; and her countenance had a mild and pleasing expression.

When brought to Fogo she was taken into the house of Mr. Leigh, the missionary, where for some time she was ill at ease, and twice during the night attempted to escape to the woods, where she would have immediately perished in the snow. She was, however, carefully watched, and in a few weeks was tolerably reconciled to her situation, and appeared to enjoy the comforts of civilization, particularly the clothes. Her own were of dressed deer-skins tastefully trimmed with martin, but she would never put them on, or part with them. She ate sparingly, disliked wine or spirits, was very fond of sleep, never getting up to breakfast before nine o'clock. She went frequently to her bedroom during the day, and when Mr. Leigh's housekeeper went up she always found her rolled in a ball in the middle of the bed apparently asleep.

At last a quantity of blue cloth was missed, and from the great jealously that Mary showed about her trunk suspicion fell upon her, her trunk was searched, and the cloth found nicely converted into sixteen pairs of mocassins which she had made in her bed. Two pairs of children's stockings were also found, made of a cotton night cap. Mr. Leigh had lost one, but Mary answered angrily about her merchandise, "John Peyton, John Peyton," meaning he had given it to her. At last, in the bottom of the trunk, the tassel of the cap and the bit marked "J.L." were found. Looking steadfastly at Mr. Leigh she pointed to her manufacture, said slowly, "Yours," and ran into the woods. When brought back she was very sulky and remained so for several weeks. The poor captive had two children and this was probably the tie that held her to her wigwam, for though she appeared to enjoy St. John's when she was taken there and her improved habits of life, she only "dragged a lengthened chain" and all her hopes and acts appeared to have a reference to her return.

She remained a short time in St. John's, and acquired such facility in speaking English that the possibility of opening a communication with her tribe through her means were hoped for, so Sir Charles Hamilton despatched Captain Buchan to the Exploits with Mary to make the attempt, so this poor devoted handful of Indians whose measure of suffering was full could at last be brought into the influence and blessings of civilization. It was otherwise. The change of dress, or change of living or whatever it may be that operates so fatally on these savages separated from their native habits, spared not poor Mary. She left St. John's with a bad cough and died of consumption on nearing the Exploits. She was twenty-four. Captain Buchan after a laborious journey reached the wigwams, but they were empty.

He left Mary's coffin there, where it was found by her people. She was ceremoniously placed by the side of her husband, the last Beothuck chieftain.

J.P. Howley
Adapted

Understanding What You Have Read

1. Why, do you think, did John Peyton rename Demasduit? Do you agree with such an action?

2. In the physical description of Demasduit, what is the dominant impression (one or two words that sums up all the phrases) created by Robinson?

3. In what ways did Demasduit maintain and display a sense of pride and dignity?

4. What does Robinson mean by the statement "she only 'dragged a lengthened chain' and all her hopes and acts appeared to have a reference to her return."?

5. What was ironic for Demasduit about (what Robinson calls) "the blessings of civilization"?

Things To Do

1. Read about the Beothucks in J.P. Howley's book from which this selection was adapted.

2. Try to discover if there are local legends about the original inhabitants in your area.

3. Plan someday to visit the Newfoundland Museum's Native Peoples display, and the Beothuck Village just west of Grand Falls.

* * *

Justin Hall

Getting Ready To Read

Here is another selection dealing with the capture and captivity of Demasduit. This time, however, the account is not historical, nor is it written from the white man's view. This time Demasduit speaks to us through the pen of a Newfoundland woman living in the second half of the twentieth century. The subjective approach is still noticeable, but is different from that of Peyton and Robinson.

Notice that the rhythm of this ballad is light and lively, even though the subject is a serious one.

The Ballad of Mary March

They will tell you if you ask them, they will tell you I am dead.
They will tell you I am lying in my cold and narrow bed.
They will tell you I am sleeping with my husband by my side,
But I wake and walk and wander and I tell you that they lied.

Many centuries ago my fathers settled here to make
Their homes about the margin of this dark and shining lake,
Where the silver-footed river from the mountains running free,
Linked us close to one another on a roadway to the sea.

The wild game of the forest gave us food and clothes to wear
There were marten, fox and otter, beaver, sable, wolf and bear;
We smoked and dried the carcasses and fashioned from the skins
All the garments that we needed — cassocks, hose and moccasins.

When I look back I wonder if the prophet could describe
The doom and devastation that were waiting for our tribe,
For the white man fell upon us like an awesome avalanche
With the grim determination to destroy us, root and branch.

Every red man was the target for some white man's deadly gun,
They relentlessly pursued us, and they shot us, one by one;
They drove us from the river and from the camp fire site,
They drove us from the hunting grounds, they stalked us day and night.

Oh my lost and stricken loved ones! I would turn away my head
From a memory that fills me with a sickness born of dread,
For the child that was abandoned and left alone to die;
For his father bruised and broken underneath that bitter sky.

They say they came in friendship but they shot him with a gun,
They stabbed him in the back and they were seven to his one;
They say they came in friendship but the child that was my own
In that dark wilderness of ice was left to die alone.

The white men took me prisoner but they could not keep me long,
For the ties that bound me to my own were rooted deep and strong.
And there is neither room nor door nor lock that can be found
To stay the captive spirit in its journey homeward bound.

And when I could no longer see or hear or feel or care
They took the empty shell of me and brought it back to where
Beneath the sullen sky upon another winter day
The tides of death came in and swept all that I loved away.

Now the wigwam is deserted and the winter winds blow through.
And nearby lies the wreckage of the little birch canoe,
But the silent trees remember and the glossy pond and lake

Still watch along the shore line in the morning when they wake;
For the vanished Indian hunter, bow and arrow in his hand,
And there is blood upon the rock and tears upon the sand.

Stella Whelan

Mrs. Whalen, was born in St. John's and worked as a provincial civil servant for 30 years. Her poems have won prizes in the Arts and Letters Competition for several years.

Understanding What You Have Read

1. What effect does the repetition of "They will tell you" have at the beginning of the poem? Who are "they"?

2. Quote from the poem to show that the writer is speaking from the Beothuck's point of view. Is there any indication that she is biased?

3. Look at the last line of the poem. Whose blood? Are the tears those of the Beothuck only? Whose else might they be? What happens to tears that fall on sand? Is that an appropriate image for this poem?

Things To Do

1. Find at least one example of each of the following in the poem:
   a) Metaphor
   b) Simile
   c) Personification
   d) Alliteration

2. Talk about the reason why the last stanza has six lines while all the others have four.

3. On a map find the Exploits River, Mary March Brook, and Red Indian Lake. Are there place name near where you live which might call to mind the Beothucks?

* * *

Getting Ready To Read

The native people of Canada have had to adjust to the ever-increasing pressure of the white man's culture. The Inuit of Labrador have learned to adapt their life-style in many ways to meet such pressures. Martin Martin suggests what the traditional values and relationships of the people were. But he also indirectly tells of the effects of the early missionaries. Can you find examples of his own confusion in defining what is purely Inuit tradition and what stems from the work of the white men in the days of his ancestors? Notice the sincerity and wisdom of this man speaking to us from his old age.

We, The Inuit, Are Changing

We, the Inuit here in Labrador, right to this day still have the traditional ways of our forefathers. Right to this day we eat what our forefathers used to eat, food with no price tags on it, food created for us ever since the earth was created. People have different foods according to their land. This I was not aware of in the past. Some eat only what is grown in gardens, others eat whatever food they can get their hands on and we, the Inuit people, have a different diet because we are people of a cold land. Because we are people of a cold land, wildlife is our main diet. Our forefathers were strong because nothing was scarce, everything was plentiful in those past years. We, the younger generation, think we are hungry but we are not because there is plenty of the white man's foods available for us to obtain at any time. We only are hungry for wildlife meat because some years are plentiful and some years there is none at all. This I have found.

Our forefather's ancestors, which we have just heard of but not seen, taught our fathers how to share any kill made amongst their people. So my father taught me to share my kill as it was the traditional way. When I was a young man every time I went hunting and came back successful I invited the poor, the less fortunate and the old Inuit to share my kill. After they had eaten they would joke around and tell stories of the past. When I heard these happy people I was aware that this was a blessing. I had made my fellow people happy through sharing. Our Creator had blessed me and I had carried on this blessing by sharing because this was meant to be. It is sad how this tradition is being forgotten. Young people now keep their kill to themselves. Some will give a little to those they wish to share with. I have said what I have seen and experienced and I am aware that this tradition is no longer practised. I hope this will be written down so that our children can be made aware of what used to take place in past years.

We have not lost all our traditions and culture yet. We have not lost our ability to hunt wildlife game. We know how to locate and hunt the game. Our young men still try to hunt in the traditional ways but they have difficulties because there is less game now. But our young Inuit have not given up trying their best to hunt for wildlife food. This we will never lose as long as there are Inuit in Labrador.

I am one hundred per cent pure Eskimo. I was never educated in the white society way because when I was a child this was not practised. Our school term lasted only six months and our main subject was studying the word of God. We had to memorize Bible verses and speak them out from memory while our teachers listened. The only time we were given a new verse was when we mastered the one before. Because of this teaching we, the elderly Inuit, can still speak out by heart many verses of the Bible, at least I always could. I don't know of my fellow elders but I'm sure they too can speak out what they memorized as children. In this generation our children have almost a whole year to learn and study but they are learning only the white society way. No wonder they have a better knowledge than we, the elderly. I am not happy that they are only being taught the white society system. I would be happy if they were taught first the word of God, then how to deal with life. I say this because I think our children don't know the true meaning of life because they refuse to hear the word of God, or are encouraged to do so. Our Inuit children are taught, I suppose, how to survive in white communities but not in the Inuit land. When learning the white society way was first introduced, or enforced, as a way of teaching our Inuit children, I strongly objected because I foresaw that in the future they would forget our Inuit language and also the word of God. I have said this because it is what I have wanted to say for ever so long. I was involved when teaching our children, then the white society way was forced on us. I was out-voted when I suggested that our children be taught the word of God first and other subjects after. I had no power to alter what was being forced on our children, my objections were not considered important. Now, what I tried to bring to attention, about our children losing their traditions and culture, is beginning to be realized by Inuit in different parts of Canada. All I have said is true. Our young Inuit have a complete new way of living and if it is let to continue, something will happen to show them they are leading a dangerous life.

In such a short time we, the Inuit of Labrador, have changed in many ways. We do not carry on many of our traditions. We are forced into many new ways which we do not even understand. Also in these days we have seen Inuit from other regions, those we had only heard about but we did not know if they had traditions and cultures which were similar to ours. Now, we see them in the flesh and see that our fellow Inuit share our traditions and culture.

Last March, when I reached the age of eighty-seven, I started to think that I had lived too long. Then another thought occurred to me, why am I still living when I am no longer able to live off the land and sea? Why am I still wandering among my fellow Inuit and being observed and told that I am no longer useful to my people? I thought once more, the Lord God has been merciful to me to this day because although I am an old man I still have a mouth which can give guidance to our younger Inuit. The years have taken their toll on me, on my hearing, my sight and my ability to walk long distances. All are no longer good and I know why this is so. When I was a young man we used to hunt caribou in the different seasons. One spring we were returning from the land when the river trails were starting to get water on the ice. Early one morning, before the sun rose, we slid from the top of the country down to a lake. The river trail had frozen over during the night and so it was usable but as the sun rose the ice melted and we began to break through into the water. When our komatiks fell through we went over knee deep in the icy water to push and pull them out. We carried on all through the day, wading, pushing, and pulling our heavily laden komatiks. My legs became so numb that I could feel nothing. Ever since that time my legs are no longer good.

I wish you peace on earth. We may never see each other on earth but through God's will we will see each other in Heaven when we are removed from the earth. So, let us look forward to meeting each other where there will be no pain or sorrow but happiness and eternal life. I am an old man now. My name is Martin Martin. I wish all a happy and successful life

Martin Martin
(Translated by William Kalleo)

Martin Martin was born in Okak, Labrador, sometime in the late years of the last century. In 1918 he moved to Nain and established among his people a reputation as an outstanding hunter and fisher. He was also highly respected for his moral and religious values, and for his service to his church as an active member, a preacher and spiritual leader. Reverend Peacock, a Moravian missionary and close friend of Martin Martin, said of him: "The singular of 'Inuit' is 'Inuk', and that word means a person of quality. Martin Martin was more than an Inuk; he was an Inumarik — a person of absolute and outstanding quality." Mr. Martin died in 1978.

Understanding What You Have Read

1. Martin Martin wishes that children could learn about their ancestors and their culture. Do you think this a common wish among other cultures? Support your answer.

2. How important is it that white people, also, be aware of Inuit traditions and culture?

3. How will it be possible to meet Martin's desire, while at the same time bringing the good things of Western civilization to his people? In your discussion refer to such things as education, communication, resource development, entertainment and social services.

Things To Do

1. Try to get a copy of "The Labrador Song" by Earl Pilgrim.

2. Find Nain on the map of Newfoundland. Locate where the settlement of Okak used to be. If you live in Nain interview people who knew Martin Martin.

3. Ask your teacher to study with you pages 19-40 of *Our Footprints Are Everywhere*, a publication of the Labrador Inuit Association.

4. Try to describe Martin Martin. Write down your description.

* * *

Simone Michel of Naskapi-Montagnais Innu Association   *David Wegenast / DECK'S AWASH*

David Wegenast / *DECK'S AWASH*

Ben Hansen

MARK-MAKERS

Some people, through outstanding qualities, have a profound effect on others. Sometimes they are individuals who are honoured and remembered. Sometimes they are groups who work together for the benefit of others. Many are forgotten, and some are never recognized.

In this unit we look at an individual, Lydia Campbell, who saw herself as a simple woman living a simple life. But through her writing we have the only record of early nineteenth century settlement of the Hamilton Inlet area. We also have preserved for us a superior personality and fine description of a way of life that had all but disappeared before this century began.

Cassie Brown displays and describes the infinite courage and totally unselfish daring of men on the Burin Peninsula, who risked their lives to save others in the colossal shipwrecks of the *Pollux* and the *Truxton* in 1942.

And we close the unit and this text with Ray Guy's tribute to all of our ancestors who taught us the values of living. Perhaps we can say that their mark was the most pervasive and indelible of all.

Getting Ready To Read

Sometime around 1892 the editor of the St. John's *Evening Herald*, Arthur Waghorne, sent an exercise book to Lydia Campbell, an elderly woman who lived in Grosswater Bay in Labrador. He asked her to write in the book "some account of Labrador life and ways." She did that, and her accounts appeared in several issues of the newspaper in 1894. Reverend Waghorne got more than he had expected, however. Lydia Campbell's writing, far from being the semi-legible scribbles of a near illiterate, proved to be a vivid and gripping account of the events of a historical period previously blank, and it was also a powerful statement of the superlative character of the woman herself. We are fortunate that this beautiful little vignette, this glimpse of the past, has been preserved for us. You will find more complete accounts in *Alluring Labrador*, published by *Them Days Magazine* in 1975, and in *Remarkable Women of Newfoundland and Labrador* presented by St. John's Local Council of Women.

To See Things And To Understand

If you wish to know who I am, I am old Lydia Campbell, formerly Lydia Brooks, then Blake, after Blake now Campbell. So, you see, ups and downs has been my life all through, and now I am what I am. Praise the Lord.

When I remember first to see things and to understand, I thought this was the only place in the world, and that my parents and sisters were the best in the world. Then our good father used to take me on his knee and tell me his home was a better country, only it was hard to live there after his good old father died . . . and he had to come out to this country to try his fortune. He and a lot more English people came out to this shore. Then, of course, they had to take wives of the natives of this country. There were very few white men here, much less women. Going ashore they found my dear, good mother and carried her off, and so it came to pass that I was one of the youngsters of them. We lived up in the riverhead, at a long bay and no one near us — more than seventy miles from anybody.

We would enjoy ourselves pretty well. There was my sister Hanna to be talking and reading with me, father and mother and an old Englishman by the name of Robert Best. Our dear father had no school book to teach us in, nothing but a family Bible and a common prayer to teach us. So we learned a little in that way.

I remember so well the day my mother died. Father met us at the door as we came from seeing our rabbit snares, with a book in his hand and told us she was dying. We all went in and kneeled down near our good mother breathing her last. By the time father was done reading and praying she was gone. Oh what did I do! Where to go! Only five of us and far from any habitation; but the Lord was with us.

When I was about twenty, I think, (I never kept account of the times or how they went) I was teaching the children of a large family, the Blakes, that I got married into. I could not write then, but I could read and teach them to read and sing hymns and to pray oft as my dear father teacht me. There were no ministers nor schoolteachers them times in this country.

Now my sister Hanna is over eighty years old and she is smart still. I have known her fighting with a wolverine, a strong animal of the size of a good sized dog. She had neither gun nor axe, but a little trout stick, yet she killed it after a long battle. It was very wicked. I wish there were more Hannas in the world for braveness.

My day's work begins before daylight, rising to make a fire, say my prayers, wash lamps, get on breakfast, sweep the house, after then I am ready with our Bible and Hymn books and prayer books on the table. So, after breakfast, I, old Lydia, seventy-five years old, puts on my outdoor clothes, takes my game bag and axe and matches, and off I goes over ice and snow, two miles or more, gets maybe three rabbits out of twenty or more snares. You may say, well done old woman, but such is life in Esquimaux Bay among a few, while some is naked and half starving for want of a little exercise.

The other day I was walking in the woods with my snowshoes on all alone looking up at the trees. At the spruce and birches looking so high and stately. I saw in the sunshine such a pretty sight above the highest trees, a flock of the beautiful white partridge, how pretty it looked and the snow glistening and the ice and trees, and me...poor old mortal...drinking in all the beautiful scenery, who will soon be out of sight but not lost, ah no, only going the way all the people has gone before.

Lydia Campbell

Lydia Campbell lived her whole life on the coast of Labrador, never had the opportunity to go to school, and yet learned to read and write quite well, and engaged in a surprising multitude of interests and activities. She was born on November 1, 1818 (although one source lists 1815) and died in 1904. She is an ancestor of Elizabeth Goudie, her sister Hanna being Mrs. Goudie's great-grandmother.

Understanding What You Have Read

1. What is there about Lydia Campbell which justifies calling her a Mark-maker?

2. What instances in this short account reveal some of the personality of this remarkable woman?

3. Can you find points of similarity between Lydia and some other Newfoundland women you have met in your reading?

Things To Do

1. Read accounts of Mrs. Campbell's diary as they appear in *From This Place* edited by Morgan, Porter and Rubia, and in the two sources listed in the introduction.

2. If you ever get to the Colonial Building in St. John's look up the copies of *The Evening Herald* for 1894 to find the original accounts.

3. Try to sketch or paint the scene described in the last paragraph, or paraphrase it as a poem.

* * *

Getting Ready To Read

Newfoundlanders who live on the coast have often witnessed sea disasters. The people of St. Lawrence and Lawn were the heroes on the fatal morning described by Cassie Brown in this excerpt from *Standing Into Danger*.

On February 18, 1942, under blizzard conditions, three American ships ran aground near St. Lawrence. The *Truxton* and the *Pollux* were battered to pieces but the *Wilkes* was able to free itself.

Two hundred and three men died in the wrecks.

Rescue At Chambers Cove

The [Iron Springs] mine had just started its early-morning shift, and Albert Grimes, the pump man, was busy checking the pumps that kept the mine dry. His boss, Rupert Turpin, the mechanical supervisor, was checking the overall mechanical operation. Rene Slaney, the mine captain, was in his office. By chance, Louis M. Etchegary, the mill superintendent, was at the mine this morning, and outside, Mike Turpin, Sylvester Edwards and Tom Beck were loading a couple of trucks with fluorspar to transport it to the mill.

It was Mike Turpin who saw the figure of a man stumbling toward them, obviously in an exhausted state. It was such an abnormal sight that the three men ran to meet him. The man was covered with a thick coating of congealed oil. "Can you help me?" he gasped.

"Yes, my son. Where do you come from?" Mike asked. He was a tall, well-set man who liked to keep his hand in fishing now and again.

The oily figure was Edward Bergeron, 18, seaman, second class. He pointed along the coast. "I've come from a war ship; she's on the rocks in a cove under cliffs. There's over 100 men on board and they need help." He added, "I came up over the cliff."

They knew that had to be Chambers Cove, and God help any ship trapped there when the wind was from the south and west, as it was today. Those who still fished gave the Chambers Cove area a wide berth on such days.

They helped the young man to the mine house, a large building with a big iron stove and a couple of rooms with tables where the miners ate their lunches and took their breaks. In a matter of minutes Louis Etchegary, Rene Slaney, Rupert Turpin and Albert Grimes gathered around the young man, who repeated his story. They knew there would be no rescue from the sea — not with the wind and waves coming around straight into the cove — and by the look of the young sailor, rescue was a matter of urgency. Mike, Syl and Tom took off immediately for the cove. Turpin carried a line.

"Get all the ropes you can find," the supervisor told Grimes.

"We'll need men," Slaney said.

"Get a few of them up out of the mine," Etchegary advised, "and phone Howard Farrell; he'll take it from there. I'll go on over to Chambers Cove." He had already looped a rope around his shoulder and was going out the door.

Slaney told Rupert Turpin, "Spread the word. Call Howard and tell everyone to get horses and sleds and get to Chambers Cove as quickly as possible. We'll go on to the cove and see if we can help."

It was rough travelling through the bush and small trees, but the distance to the cove was considerably less. In little more than a half-hour they reached the ravine and the hayshed. Mike counted four men, black with fuel, huddled under a coating of hay. "Are you all right?" he asked.

"We're all right," one answered, "but there are others on the beach and on the ship."

The three men hurried up the hill and stood on the clifftop. Wind, spray, and sleet drove at them so fiercely they had to shield their eyes against it. To a man who had been born and brought up close to the sea, the *Truxton* was a heart-wrenching sight. Sleek, gleaming, her big guns ready for action, she looked beautiful but pitiful as she lay at a 45 degree angle between. . .two rocks with the seas exploding over her. At least 100 men were clinging to the safety lines on her port side. White water cascaded into the cove, breaking upon the edge of the oil slick that extended 30 feet from the shore. Wreckage and life rafts heaved and tossed in the oil strung from the ship, and sailors were clinging to the flotsam*. As the wreckage overturned, or was torn from their grasp, the sea swept them toward the cliff.

Where Bergeron. . .had come up, there was a light handline looped around a knob of ice. Mike picked it up. He would not trust it to hold around the ice. "You stay here, Tom, and hold onto the rope. Syl and I will go down to the beach," he told Tom Beck.

Tom stationed himself on the incline, well back from the cliff's edge, and grasped the rope while Mike eased down the slippery cliff to the beach below, making use of the holes chopped in the ice by Bergeron. He could not help but marvel at the daring and endurance of the young sailor who had hacked his way to the top. Syl Edwards followed. There were a few men in the water close to the beach and Mike waded out to his hips, threw them a line and hauled them in. Minutes later, Louis Etchegary came to the clifftop, and he, too, worked his way down the cliff while Tom Beck held the line.

Ensign Frederick Loughridge and his bedraggled, frozen men, cramped into the recess at the far end of the beach, were overjoyed at seeing the Newfoundland men. "Thank God!" Loughridge said fervently.

"Help is coming," Louis Etchegary told him, "more men and ropes, and horses and sleds."

"The captain will be happy to know that," Loughridge said, and ordered Signalman Parkerson to signal the *Truxton* that help was on the way.

Word of the disaster spread very quickly. Theo Etchegary, the strapping 28-year-old chemist at the mill (and son of Louis, the mill superintendent) received the news in a phone call from an excited Rupert Turpin, and spread the news to the merchants in the community; then he commandeered a truck driven by young Alan Farrell, whose helper was Theo's 16-year-old brother Gus, and the three took off for the Iron Springs Mine. The merchants took it from there, alerting the townspeople.

At the mine, Theo paused long enough to collect a stout rope, but Gus and Alan, impatient to see the action, took off like a couple of deer. A young fellow, Charlie Brinston, followed Theo as he set out across the hills, but he was quickly left behind.

Captain Tom Connors of the *SS Kyle* put to sea and steamed along the coast to Chambers Cove in an attempt to effect rescue from the sea.

Halfway to Chambers Cove, Theo met Rene Slaney and Rupert Turpin, with a couple of blackened, oil-soaked survivors they had met wandering across the hills. Harry Egner and Lanier Phillips had emphasized the gravity of the situation, and Slaney and Turpin were going back to the mine to get more men.

"I'll go on," Theo said, and presently he came upon the oil-smeared shed in the ravine and, hearing voices, he poked his head inside. "Don't stay here and freeze; walk to the mine. It's not far," he told the shivering sailors. "There'll be food and clothes for you when you get there."

The sailors made no move to leave. "There's nothing you can do here, and there's plenty of help coming for your friends," Theo said. "It's better for you to start walking; at least it'll keep you warm."

The men got stiffly to their feet, stumbled out of the shed and moved clumsily up the side of the ravine. "It's not far," Theo called, then he climbed the hill to where the lone figure of Tom Beck was keeping vigil.

It was difficult to look into the teeth of the wind laden with sleet, spray and splatterings of oil, but Theo's eyes were drawn to the huge warship heeled over on the rocks, the seas smothering her, the men clinging to her port railing. Straight out, along the coast a mile or more he saw another ship (The *USS Wilkes*) standing off. He did not question in his mind what a ship was doing there, but he knew it would be of no assistance to the one trapped below.

In the heaving water between the ship and shore, a few sailors, like tiny black bubbles in the gummy oil, were trying to cling to a couple of rafts of wreckage, but the waves swept everything from their grasp. One man tried to crawl aboard a raft but it tipped and slid away. He disappeared for a long moment, then popped up and made another try. It was a painful sight to watch, and Theo, wasting no more time, took his coil of rope, passed it to Tom Beck to hold onto, and prepared to lower himself over the edge.

Beck, shouting above the uproar, told him, "Your dad and Gus are down on the beach."

"All right," Theo called back. By the time he had worked his way down the cliff, more sailors had made their way to the shore, had been hauled upon the beach, and were being forced to their feet to keep moving. All of them were exhausted from cold and exposure. Theo put his jacket around a scantily clad youngster. One sailor had lost his shoes and socks and one of the Newfoundland men removed his own warm woolly socks, put his rubber boots back on his bare feet, then knelt and put his socks on the feet of the young man.

The combined noise of the wind roaring into the cove and the seas hammering the cliffs was overwhelming, and the tide would shortly be at its peak, leaving only a strip of five or six feet of beach for them to work from.

Ensign Loughridge explained the abortive attempt to get the life rafts and the lifeline back to the ship, and Theo, Sylvester and Mike immediately began a search of the shore for the line, while Louis Etchegary ordered young Gus to gather fuel for a fire. The wet, frozen men were reeling from exhaustion, and Loughridge had to speak sharply to them to keep them on the move.

Gus scrounged around the rocks and crevices, picking up pieces of driftwood and wreckage that had been thrown up on the beach, including an oil-soaked life jacket. After a great deal of difficulty, a smoky fire was lit, and although it gave little heat, it perked the men up and they shuffled over to it. All except one, a youth very little older than Gus, who lay on the shingle.

"Get him moving, Gus," Louis Etchegary ordered his son. Like the other Newfoundlanders he was busy dragging around a survivor himself. Gus went to the young man, knelt, and put his arm around him. "Come on," he encouraged, and carted him to the fire. Round and round they walked. "What's your name?" Gus asked.

"Butterworth. Bill Butterworth," the youth mumbled, his body shaking with weakness and cold.

It struck Gus that this was no mere adventure; this was

stark truth, life and death, and total involvement in it. Heedless of the wind and sleet on his own body, Gus took off the old jacket with a sheepskin lining that he was wearing and put it around Butterworth. "It'll keep you warm," he said. Presently he had to leave the youth to search the shoreline for more firewood.

By now more men had arrived from the mine and worked their way down the cliff to the beach, making it very crowded. Among them were Abe Pike, Leo Loder, Henry Lambert, Dave Edwards, George Carr, Fred Walsh, Neil Tarrant, Charlie Pike, Arch Pike, Alfred Turpin, Phil Edwards, and Gregory Edwards (who would later write a song about the shipwreck). Dozens of other men were gathering on the top of the cliff, ready to give a hand in any way they could.

Theo and his two companions had slogged through the muck along the shore, but found no line. They could see the fouled life rafts about 50 feet off from the beach, but closer, at the edge of the oil slick, was the raft the men had been trying to climb onto. It was still in the same position, twisting and turning, appearing and disappearing as oil waves engulfed it.

Theo yelled above the din: "If the raft's got a rope attached to the ship, we might be able to free it and then we'll have a contact with the ship. Do you think we can haul it back to the beach?" If they could possibly get a line from ship to shore, there need not be any further loss of life; no need for those desperate men to try to swim that treacherous stretch of water.

Sylvester Edwards was a fearless man. "We can try, if you like."

The waves in which the raft was bouncing were running four and five feet and it would not be easy to control. Theo and Sylvester tied ropes around their waists and, as their companions held the other end, began to wade out to it. The scum of oil was about a foot deep and so tough they could barely get through it. The frigid water burned as it crept up their legs, thighs and bodies, then mercifully numbed them. The bottom of the cove, farther out, was rocky and rough, and they felt their way carefully, Theo ignoring the alarmed shouts of his father. Soon the waves were rolling over their shoulders but they reached the raft, only to find it firmly snagged to the bottom. They tugged at it, trying to drag it toward the shore, but it bounced and dipped, and stayed where it was. Because of the thickness of the oil, they dared not explore beneath the raft, and . . . they had to return to the beach without it. They continued to range back and forth along the shoreline, searching for the lifeline which, they reasoned, could be snagged on rocks closer to the shore. At the same time they kept a close watch on the *Truxton*, waiting for her men to make the first move. They could do nothing until then. A feeling of helplessness and inadequacy swept over them.

Theo made his way out onto a ledge on the base of the pink cliff and saw the *SS Kyle* backing cautiously to within 500 yards of the entrance to the cove, but the seas were huge and the ship could go no farther. It was foreboding. If Captain Connors couldn't help it was certain no other ship could. Wisely Connors steamed back to St. Lawrence harbor, where he ordered his crew to gather ropes, axes, and ships' blankets and get overland to Chambers Cove.

Gus went to find more firewood and when he returned he discovered young Butterworth lying dead on the beach. "You may as well put on your jacket, Gus," one man advised. "He dropped a little while ago."

Gus did not know Butterworth, and their brief association did not warrant any personal feeling, but he had felt a kinship with the young man and in a gush of emotion he wept as he tended the fire. As cold as he was, he could not bring himself to take his jacket from the young sailor . . . not yet.

There was enough manpower on the top now to start bringing the survivors up the cliff. They were in no condition to work their way up by themselves, not even with ropes strapped around them, but that problem was not difficult to solve. The ice would permit them to be more or less slid up the cliff. A rope strap was hitched under the arms of the first man, and with seven or eight men hauling on the line, the limp form was eased over the glistening surface without any apparent difficulty. Yet there were protuberances* on the cliff of ice, and he was bruised and bleeding when he came over the top. He was immediately taken to the shed in the ravine to await the arrival of a horse and sled to take him to Iron Springs. The second man was also battered by the time he reached the top. Someone went down the rope to tell them what was happening, and there was a consultation.

There was only one other possibility and that was on the other side of the craggy little cliff jutting out into the sea. The miners were familiar with the ravine there; they would have to use it to carry the survivors to the top. It meant literally carrying the men over the smaller cliff as well.

"Let's get 'em up," Abe Pike said to Mike Turpin.

Aided by George Carr, they began their backbreaking task. With the survivors on their shoulders they made their way over the small cliff into the next cove; then they strapped a rope around themselves and the sailors and, digging their toes in on either side of the narrow ravine, they inched their way up. It was easy on the survivors — but killing work on the rescuers.

Cassie Brown

Cassie Brown was born in Rose Blanche on the South West Coast of Newfoundland. Before becoming an author she worked as a journalist. Her published works are **Death on the Ice: The Great Newfoundland Sealing Disaster of 1914. A Winter's Tale: The Wreck of the Florizel. Standing Into Danger: A Dramatic Story of Shipwreck and Rescue.**

Understanding What You Have Read

1. Study a good map of the Burin Peninsula on the south coast of Newfoundland to find the exact location of the wreck.

2. There are many incidents of bravery described in this selection. Which do you feel is most outstanding? Why is that?

3. Many of the young men in this story were not much older than high school students. Think about and discuss with others in your class the relationship between Gus Etchegary and Bill Butterworth. Can you explain the intensity of young Etchegary's feelings?

Things To Do

1. This excerpt describes the *Truxton* in Chambers Cove. Find out where the *Pollux* went aground and draw a sketch map of the area marking in the towns, the wrecks, the overland routes used, and the wind and tide directions.

2. This is a true story. Cassie Brown's research is so painstaking that every incident, every conversation, can be substantiated. Borrow *Standing Into Danger* from your library and read more of this fascinating account.

* * *

Ben Hansen

Getting Ready To Read

Tributes in the House of Assembly to the memory of
Hon. John T. Cheeseman, member for Hermitage, who
died in February, 1968, prompted this short comment by
Ray Guy. In it he reminds us that our heritage is made up
of more than historical events, material things, stories
and songs. See if you can find the one sentence which
sums up what our Uncle Johns have left us.

Uncle John

All I know of Mr. Cheeseman is what I saw and heard of him
during his last two years in the House.

He wore a waistcoat with a watch chain across it. He had
snow-white hair, and I judged by his face that he must have
made a splendid grandfather and uncle.

His eyes were merry and dimmed only when he spoke of the
hardships and trials endured by the people of his isolated south
coast district.

Mr. Cheeseman must have been known as "Uncle John" to
a wide circle of people outside his own family.

It is a Newfoundland custom to show respect to the older
men of the community by calling them "uncle" — whether they
are related to you or not.

My favorite honorary uncle is also named John. He is 85
years old or more. He has seen many hardships and sorrows in
his time and they still continue.

He is a short man who has round, rosy cheeks and smokes a
pipe, but the thing he is best known for is telling "yarns."

Sometimes he can't remember things that happened a
month ago but he can recall in perfect detail things that
happened before this century was born.

He may start a yarn, "The other year when the Boer War
was on . . ." or "I mind the time when the States was dry and we
went down to Saint Peter's . . ."

The remarkable thing is that all of his hundreds of stories
are jolly. Having lived through what we sometimes hear were
wretched and bitter times, he seems to recall only the jokes and
the anecdotes and the bright parts.

"A time to laugh and a time to cry." Uncle John has discovered along the way how to subtract from the one and add to the other.

There are thousands of "Uncle Johns" in Newfoundland. Perhaps they wonder if they'll leave us anything to remember them by but a few amusing stories?

Theirs was another age. Maybe they think they have nothing valid or of value to leave to this new generation?

They need not worry. They have shown us that the worst of times may be survived, that hardships may be overcome, that sorrows pass . . . and that at the end of the trip, the good parts are what we will remember best.

Do not think you leave us, Uncles, with no remembrance of you. You have shown us how to live. That is your monument and your memorial and it will last far longer than stone.

Ray Guy

Understanding What You Have Read

1. Use quotations to show that Mr. Guy thought that the Hon. John T. Cheeseman was a senstive and sympathetic man.

2. How does this man remind Ray Guy of another Uncle John?

3. What characteristics of this second Uncle John are to be found in the "thousands of Uncle Johns" found in the province?

4. In your own words say what all these Uncle Johns have left us.

5. Why does Ray Guy say that what they have left us will last far longer than stone?

Things To Do

1. Read the last selection in each of *You May Know Them As Sea Urchins, Ma'am* and *That Far Greater Bay*, both by Ray Guy. Would you say that Mr. Guy shares a common characteristic with the Uncle Johns? What would it be?

2. See the biographical note on Ray Guy at the end of "A Turn In My Road" on p.11.

* * *

Ben Hansen

accost / vb.   come up and speak to
animate / vb.   to give life to; to make lively
astuteness / n.   shrewdness, discernment
audacious / adj.   bold; daring
augment / vb.   increase; enlarge
bigotry / n.   prejudice; intolerance
bilious / adj.   sickly
bludgeon / vb.   to strike with a club; to bully
bracken / n.   large coarse weedy ferns occurring in meadows,
                woods and especially wastelands
callous / adj.   hard; hardened
canvas / n.   strong cloth made of cotton; flax or hemp used
                for sails
Cape Ann / n.   head covering for fishermen, usually of black
                rubber or yellow oil cloth
carrion / n.   dead and decaying flesh
catapult / vb.   to throw back; hurl
comber / n.   a wave which rolls over or breaks at the top
commiserate / vb.   feel or express sorrow for
concavity / n.   an inwardly curved object or form
concession / n.   anything yielded; a privilege granted
                by a government, company, etc.
contumacy / n.   stubborn resistance to authority
consternation / n.   great alarm or dismay; paralyzing fear
cull / vb.   to pick out; select
drogue / n.   see definition below - spelling varies
droke / n.   in Newfoundland a thick clump of woods usually in a valley
earmark/ vb.   identify or give information about; to set aside
                for a special purpose
elide / vb.   to omit or slur over in pronunciation
embalm / vb.   to treat a dead body to keep it from decaying
enshrine / vb.   to keep sacred; cherish
flotsam / n.   odds and ends floating on the water; debris
gimlet / n.   small tool with a screw point for boring holes
ground swell / n.   broad deep wavesby a distant storm
grump / n.   an iron post on a wharf used for tying on boats
hag-down / n.   a large salt water bird
health-cultist / n.   a person who has great admiration or
                worship for health
hogshead / n.   a large barrel
killick / n.   in Newfoundland a homemade anchor (large rocks
                enclosed by a wooden frame)
longevity / n.   long life
lore / n.   facts and stories about a certain subject

mawsy / adj.   dull, dreary (i.e. a mawsy day)

meningitis / n.   a serious disease affecting the three membranes surrounding the brain and spinal column

metronome / n.   a timing device which can be adjusted to tick at different speeds (used generally by persons practicing musical instruments to help keep time)

metropolitan / adj.   of a large city or belonging to a large city

mettle / n.   disposition; temperament

minis / n.   short dresses or skirts

mollified / adj.   softened, pacified

morose / adj.   gloomy, sullen, ill-humoured

nocturnal / adj.   active at night

paltry / adj.   trivial, small

paucity / n.   smallness of number or quantity

perceptible / adj.   noticeable

piss-a-bed / n.   in Newfoundland a common name for dandelion

prating / vb.   chattering foolishly

protocol / n.   a code of diplomatic procedure or etiquette; a strict code of manners

protuberance / n.   a rough bulge

puncheon m/   an extra large cask or barrel

regurgitate / vb.   to vomit

satirize / vb.   to use wit, irony or sarcasm to expose vice or folly

skeptic / n.   one who has a critical or doubting attitude

skig / n.   that part of the keel of a boat extending below the propeller to which the rudder is attached

sunkers / n.   dangerous rocks, usually near shore, which may be partially submerged

swells / n.   large waves

temper / vb.   to soften or dilute by the addition of something else

tidewaiter / n.   an old word for customs officer

undertow / n.   the current beneath the surface that goes seaward from waves breaking upon shore

vamps / n.   in Newfoundland short hand-knit socks made from homespun wool

vestryman / n.   a member of a group in a church responsible for robes, altar linens, sacred vessels, etc.

ACKNOWLEDGMENTS

MRS. KOLLIN by Grace Butt. Reprinted by permission of the editors of *From This Place* (Jesperson Printing Ltd.) 1977.

MACDONALD'S PLAIN by Enos Watts. From *After the Locusts* (Breakwater Books Ltd.) 1974.

THE GHOST SHIP. From *Fish & Brewis, Toutens & Tales* by Len Margaret (Breakwater Books) 1980.

LET ME FISH OFF CAPE ST. MARY'S by Otto P. Kelland. Reprinted by permission of the author.

MY POLITICAL CAREER. From *My Newfoundland* by A.R. Scammell (Harvest House) 1966.

AS LOVED OUR FATHERS by Thomas Cahill. Reprinted by permission of the author.

STORM COMING, WINTER AFTERNOON and NOAH. From *Hemlock Cove and After* by Tom Dawe.

A TURN IN MY ROAD and UNCLE JOHN by Ray Guy. Reprinted by permission of the author.

OLD MAN ORDERING TEA by Mary Dawe (Sharpe). Reprinted by permission of the author.

THE BALLAD OF MARY MARCH by Stella Whelan. From *From This Place* (Jesperson Printing Ltd.) 1977.

CURTAINS by Percy Janes. Reprinted by permission of the author and *The Newfoundland Quarterly*.

RESCUE AT CHAMBERS COVE. From *Standing into Danger* by Cassie Brown (Doubleday Canada Limited) 1979

The publisher has made every reasonable effort to contact copyright holders of materials in this book. We would be pleased to be advised of any errors or omissions.

* * *

Thanks to Colleen Lynch of the **Department of Rural Development — Craft Division** *for information on and use of the cover photograph*